On The Indian Trail

On The Indian Trail

By

A. Lyle Van Dyne, M.D.

GYAN

Published by

Gyan Publishing House
5, Ansari Road
Daryaganj, New Delhi-110002
Phone: 011-47034999, 9811692060
E-mail: books@gyanbooks.com

Distribution Network
gyanbooks.com
India, USA, Canada, UK, Australia, France

ISBN: 978-81-212-7781-5 (PB)
First Published, 1921

2nd Impression 2023

Printed at: Gyan Press, Delhi.

ON THE INDIAN TRAIL
Author: A. LYLE VAN DYNE

On The Indian Trail

By

A. Lyle Van Dyne, M.D.

Printed for the Author
By
The Abingdon Press, Chicago

On The Indian Trail

Written by A. L. Van Dyne

CHAPTER I

THE AWAKENING

In the gray mists of early dawn, Ahwaha awakened from a strange dream. Bending over her, she had seen her Indian mother and heard her say, "Daughter, maybe you found riches and high position with your white friends, but you have forgotten your poor Indian mother. I loved and nursed you for a long time, Ahwaha, now I am sad because you have forgotten me."

Ahwaha raised her slender body and sat upright upon her bed. "Riches and honor!" she sadly whispered, "Ah, no! dear mother. I found love that has caused my heart to bleed; I found sorrow and weakness and I have found my soul. I am going back to you, mother, and our people. Now I know that even Ahwaha has work to do. Dr. Martel many times said, 'Ahwaha, you are brave and strong.' Yesterday I saw them place his ashes in the cold ground. Now I have only his kind words to sustain me."

At that moment she recalled the little box which the doctor had given to her on the very night of his sudden, terrible illness.

"Do not open the box, Ahwaha," he had said, "until I am gone."

Ahwaha knelt down before the little black trunk at the foot of her bed and reverently drew out the box from beneath piles of folded clothing. She felt that the doctor was close beside her. She lifted the cover and there lay a small white envelope addressed in his own hand—"To Ahwaha, who has been my comfort and support through hours of nameless agony." Great, hot tears fell over the little white envelope from the dark eyes of the Indian girl.

Many minutes passed before she could uncover the last message from the man she loved and mourned. Very timidly she drew out the folded sheet of elegant paper and read through her tears, "Ahwaha—dear child of Nature: You can never know how much you have comforted me. You are so calm and brave. After all, Ahwaha, a loving, pure friendship is the highest possession of this life. It brings no pangs of remorse, no terrible complications, no wreckage. Dear child, go back to your people. Until I knew your heart, I thought the Indian a worthless, hopeless creature. But in you, Ahwaha, I find a rare intelligence, a rare soul, a deep, sensitive, intricate nature. I now believe that the Indian's great need is to find himself. Ahwaha, help them as you have helped me. May Heaven shower upon you all the good that can come to any mortal. Accept the little gift I here enclose, with my heart. —To Ahwaha, from Eugene Martel."

Down at the bottom of the box, folded carefully, in a white linen handkerchief Ahwaha found ten one hundred dollar bills. In all her life she had never seen so much money. But so deep was her grief she could not sense the value of this gift. "I will go back to my people, as he commanded me," she sobbed. "And with me I take knowledge that cannot be imparted by books, for I have learned that success, and happiness, do not depend upon money, nor talent, nor position, nor marvelous personal gifts, for Dr. Martel had all these and much more. Here, in this magnificent home, I have witnessed a prince descend into the depths of Hades, because the laws of Nature are relentless, unchangeable, eternal, and my precious friend paid the price. Great God, help me to hold up the torch of Truth to my people."

One hour later, Ahwaha said to a gaunt, haggard-eyed woman who descended from the top floor, "I am going away—going back to my mother and my father. I shall leave to-day."

They looked at each other and the haggard woman said, "No doubt that is a wise thing for you to do, Ahwaha. Take with you all the furnishings of this room. There are such loads of stuff in this house I do not know what to do with it."

There were some things in her little room which Ahwaha loved—a tiny writing-desk, placed there by Dr. Martel when she came, three small pictures, and a half dozen books he had put on the walls and the desk. She thanked the pale mistress of the house between broken sobs. She would take everything away with her. It would enable her to transplant a bit of the doctor's life into her Indian home. She would build a shrine where their spirits would meet before this little desk. With a feeling of reverence she removed the pretty curtains from the window, lifted the rug from the floor, packed the books and pictures, and one small bust of Wagner. Dr. Martel had placed the little bust upon a shelf in the corner. Ahwaha ran to the room where the doctor died. She laid her head upon the couch where his had lain in its last sleep. She closed her eyes and whispered, "I will try! I am only a poor Indian girl, but I will try, and your spirit will go with me and sustain me." Hot tears fell from her eyes. Then suddenly, she said aloud, "I am weak and helpless, and the doctor called me strong and brave. He trusted me and leaned upon me."

She arose and said in a firm voice, "He is not gone! He is here! He will walk beside me and I shall hear his voice because this is a world of our own making, a world of thought."

The pale-faced woman had gone out without bidding Ahwaha farewell, but in the lower hall she met the old housekeeper, who said, "Well, good-by, little Indian girl." And then, suddenly, the door of the great house closed for the last time upon Ahwaha.

CHAPTER II

THE RETURN

Ahwaha returned to her Indian home on a cool, bright spring day. There was gladness in the air, and everything looked fresh and green. Half an hour before the train reached the little town adjoining the reservation, a terrific thunderstorm had swept down from the northeast and left everything clean and sparkling in the sunlight. It only lasted a few moments, but in that time it had carried away a section of the track and the train was stalled just outside and in full view of the village. Over the prairie the people came straggling, curious to learn what had happened. Ahwaha sprang down into the wet sand and the conductor placed her hand baggage upon the ground beside her. At that moment a tall, young Indian approached and lifting his hat, inquired in low tones, "May I assist you with your baggage, miss?" The man, although a stranger, belonged to her people. That was quite obvious. Ahwaha replied, "Yes, you are very kind. They did not expect me home. We live up on the river bank. You may go with me beyond the village. Maybe father will come to meet me. His eyes are alert for strangers upon the path."

The young man had caught up the heavy luggage and was swinging along with the natural ease and grace of the Red Man. Ahwaha followed in silence, through the town and out across the fields where the path was flanked by huge beds of blue crocuses. As they neared the river, Ahwaha's companion turned and looked back, for he no longer heard her footsteps. He saw the Indian girl kneeling upon the ground, with both hands pressed over her eyes. Stepping softly, Tonto Cabo went back along the path. When he reached Ahwaha, he stood staring at the blue flowers until she sprang to her feet and said, "It is nothing, only my friend loved the crocus." This was true, but there was something more. Ahwaha had reached a curve in the path, from which point she saw her Indian home, and there upon the doorstep sat her mother, with her tangled hair falling about her shoulders and her bare feet protruding from beneath a soiled and ragged calico skirt; and the poor girl cowered before this vision of reservation life. But the doctor's face came between, and suddenly all her strength and courage returned.

Tonto Cabo was not a reservation Indian. He looked upon the girl's daintily clad figure and into her great, dark eyes, and understood. Ahwaha stammered, "You are kind and good, but mother is coming to help me. Go now."

She ran toward the Indian woman who took her in her arms and held her close to her breast. The mother was comely to look upon, in spite of the fact that her outward appearance contrasted sharply with that of the daughter, who had returned from the great city in smart attire. Tonto dropped the heavy luggage in the path, turned back and glided along toward the village. As he walked, he mused —"She is the daughter of Chief Thunder Bird. That is well. I shall meet him at nightfall and talk about the land and see his pretty daughter." But when the night descended, and the moon climbed toward the zenith, Thunder Bird went down the path to meet Tonto and led him to the river bank, where they sat down upon a mound of earth and talked of tribal matters, far into the night.

When they parted the old Chief said, "You will come back in three moons. Then you will see Ahwaha and hear her sing like the birds."

In the morning Tonto went away, and to the distant city he carried the memory of Ahwaha's beautiful face and gentle sadness. To the birds in the city park he whispered, "I will go back and hear her sing."

When the second day dawned, Ahwaha was up with the birds. She saw the sun rise and bathe the earth in rose and gold. She heard a thousand bird voices hail the day. She walked out among the Indian shanties; not a window or door was open. "Sealed up tight to keep out this glorious morning air, and light, and color," Ahwaha said aloud. Then she walked away up the river, drinking in all the beauty and life poured out so lavishly about her. When beyond the little settlement, she sang just for the joy of singing, just because she felt herself a part of the beautiful morning. Then slowly she retraced her steps, and as she walked she planned what she would do to better the life of the people existing in the dirty little hovels, without even the air and sunlight, for every opening was carefully fastened. The thought came to Ahwaha—"this life is not the normal life of the Indian. They shifted their homes often and the wind swept through the lodges at will in the old times; I see; I know; it all came about through the changed way of living."

She went back to the house, and with her own hands removed the window from her sleeping room. The old Chief had built a substantial frame cottage on the bank of the river near the bridge, over which the footpath led to the little settlement in the woods. The grass was a pale, bright green, and the cottage had received a fresh coat of bright, blue paint.

For two days Ahwaha counseled with her parents; but on the evening of the third day all the Indians of the little settlement, and some from beyond the grove several miles distant, came to a council-fire lighted to welcome Ahwaha. Beyond the river, the road climbed up a steep hill. Near the top of the hill a path led off to the right, through the woods, and into a small clearing. Here the Indians had built their shanties and log huts in a circle, close to the trees, on the border of the clearing.

In the center the council-fire was built. Chief Thunder Bird sat facing the east, before the fire. At his right, in a semi-circle, were huddled the men and boys. At his left, sat all the women and children, with Ahwaha nearest to himself. The women had donned their beads and trinkets, and allowed their hair to fall in long braids, and Ahwaha arrayed herself like all the other maidens. After Chief Thunder Bird had addressed the gathering in their native tongue, the Indian girls sang and danced the Peace Dance, in the weird light of the council-fire. Then Ahwaha told them of the white man's ways, and of their dances, and then she said, "I have returned to you with love and sorrow, and peace and hope in my heart. Come to me, dear friends. Perhaps I may help you. That is my wish. I have received much light. I have suffered. I came back because a good spirit commanded me to come to my people. Much that the white man has is not civilization, but simply commercialism. We must choose the good, the best. The Indian race is forced to let go the old life. That is gone. The life we live now, here on the reservation is not so good as the old life—not so natural—not so clean—not so full of romance and mystery, and hope. The change has already occurred, and we had nothing to do with that. What I say to you is, Get the best or we are lost. Health and happiness are life's greatest gifts."

"There, that will do," Chief Thunder Bird commanded. "I see our people someones understand not. That much heap good, but too much said."

He beckoned to a tall, dark Indian girl, and all the maidens came forward and laid upon the ground before Ahwaha, little gifts of beadwork and baskets. Some were useful, others ornamental, but all were fashioned by the hands that bore them.

"See," continued Chief Thunder Bird, "this much more good than talk. Our children go among the whites, then they come back and speechify. Sing, Ahwaha, sing. That more good."

And while the older women brought food and served each guest, Ahwaha sang the songs she had learned at Carlisle. Then the big fire burned low, and the black shadows stretched far behind the dusky figures. The red glow flared up over the dark faces, died down, flamed up again, and then again more feebly, until there was no light save that from the moon, and one by one the Indians disappeared.

CHAPTER III

The Reservation

Tonto came back; came to counsel with Chief Thunder Bird; came to hear Ahwaha sing; came to court the Wild Flower, who during his absence had patiently tried to help her people. He found the home of Thunder Bird changed from a squalid, dreary place into a habitation that might have held the soul of an artist. Ahwaha had made good use of the furnishings brought from the home of her friend in the city. The low walls were adorned with choice pictures. She had draped the doors with old faded blankets, but they were clean and soft-toned in color. She had hung the mounted deer-heads above the doors, spread the Indian mats and rugs where the colors blended best, made with her own hands a book-rack, placed it against the wall of the living-room and filled it with books. She had made a den for Chief Thunder Bird, decorated with Indian relics, where the old Chief could smoke and dream and relate his old-time stories.

When Tonto first visited Chief Thunder Bird, not a tree, or shrub, or flower, grew about the house. Now the whole place was abloom with green and flowering things, and here and there young trees were planted. At the rear of the dwelling, a big vegetable garden flourished. Ahwaha had also purchased a cow and a large flock of chickens. "Bravo," cried Tonto, "someone is thinking, someone is working, about this place, and the result is wonderful." "I bought the chickens," Ahwaha explained, "because the old lady who lives just beyond the bridge came home one day from the village lugging a dead hen, one that had died from disease and been cast over the fence by the owner. I could not prevent her eating that diseased fowl, but now I give her one every week, and she weeds in the garden for a couple of hours in payment." "Fine, fine!" cried Tonto, "I have found a real Princess—a woman who thinks. Our people do not comprehend that without material possessions one is helpless. We must surround ourselves with necessities, with comforts, and beauty."

Ahwaha replied, "Yes, even the little squirrels teach this lesson of thrift and reserve supply. Material possessions give power and prestige. In the old days our people were rich in furs, blankets, baskets, etc. But a blight has fallen upon them. Now poverty and helplessness and disease cry out from all the reservation homes. It is all because of the changed life." "I hate the Pale Face," Tonto said. Then he turned upon his heel, returned to the house and said to Chief Thunder Bird, "You said that I should hear Ahwaha sing." "Yes, yes, the lark sing now but not so much. She think all time." He called to his daughter and from a peg on the wall she took down the old guitar and sang, low, sad, minor melodies. Then she and Tonto sang together. They sang the old songs they had learned at Carlisle, afterward they talked of their old school days. "O, those were glorious days," Ahwaha murmured, "and the good Dr. Nachita, was he there at that time? Did you know him?" Tonto eagerly questioned. "Yes, I never could forget Dr. Nachita. He gave us the pills and powders and said, 'Take care of yourself. Don't get sick. Understand, if you do, I must give you bad medicine.' We owe much to Carlisle." Chief Thunder Bird beckoned Tonto and again they went to a lonely spot on the bank of the river, where they remained until the sun had set and the big moon sailed out into the blue heavens.

On the following morning the east was flushed with pink and gold, and the long, gray shadows lay over the green earth, when Tonto rowed up the river from the village. At the bridge he ran the nose of his canoe on the bank and waited—not long—for Ahwaha was watching and ran down the hillside and stepped into the bow of the boat. Chief

Thunder Bird had given permission for them to go up-stream and pass the day at the agency, several miles north from his little settlement. For a long time no word passed between the man and woman in the boat. They listened to the swish of the oars through the water, and the voices of the birds. They watched the banks of rose, and gray, and gold clouds piled up in the east. The river was fringed with silver poplars and willows and pines. The current was not rapid. Tonto's arms were long and sinewy and the canoe sped swiftly onward until they reached a little cove filled with white lilies, and little green, boggy tufts, or hillocks. Tonto turned the boat into this harbor away from the current of the stream and there rested for a time, while Wild Flower broke the lilies from the stalks and laid them at her feet in the canoe. Few words had passed between them, for all nature was singing to them in soft, clear tones. The little yellow and blue warblers and the cat-bird filled the air with sweet sounds, and the flowers shook their heads and filled the air with fragrance. The blue sky and the fleecy white clouds said, "Come up higher where the air is clear and cool," but the canoe rocked upon the water, and Tonto said, "Wild Flower, are you happy here among your people?" "Well," the girl replied, "everything is beautiful. Everything is harmonious and full of life and joy except the people. Tonto, my heart is heavy. Something is wrong. I do not understand. They dance and shout and laugh, but it is not for joy. It is for diversion, to forget their utterly hopeless condition."

Tonto looked into the eyes of Ahwaha and felt that a great change was taking place in her. "Come away from this place, Wild Flower," he whispered, "come back to the city. Come with me and be my song-bird and I will make you happy, child." She pulled the white petals from a full-blown lily and threw them into the water. She watched them float beyond her reach. Still she was silent. "You have been out into the big world where people think and act for themselves. You cannot live here, Wild Flower. The social and mental atmosphere will stifle you." "Ah, Tonto," the girl replied, "what you say is true, but I gave my promise and it is sacred. Then, too, mother is far from well. She sits silent and motionless for hours. She never speaks with strangers, and her words are few when alone with the family. She has a wasting disease. I cannot leave her. I have a double trust. When you come again, Tonto, I will give you my answer. My life here is very busy. I find much to accomplish, but I stand apart from my own people. They look upon me as one out of sympathy with their interests, one trying to teach them new tricks. Many times I find it necessary to do as they do in order to have the least influence with them or be admitted into their circle."

"Yes, Ahwaha, I see this change. They are dragging you down to their level in speech and appearance. You must come with me. Before the snow falls I will come back and take you to my home."

"O, Tonto, we must be going now. We have lingered a long time in this pretty nook."

A frightened look passed over her face.

Tonto grasped the oars, plunged them into the water, pulled hard and steady and away shot the canoe up stream.

When they reached the agency a dance was in full swing. Close to the river where the air was cool a large company of Indian men and women were jumping and whirling upon the bare ground, accompanied by weird sounds from the tom-tom. On the ground sat old women, with gay-colored blankets piled all about them. Others were beading moccasins or making finger rings.

Tonto joined the dancers, but Wild Flower lingered among the baskets and purchased many pretty trinkets. Afterward she made her way to the lodge of the great medicine man and told him of her sick mother. About the old, weather-beaten, grizzled Red Man there was a wealth of mystery and quiet dignity. He closed his eyes and sat in silence for a long time, then he spoke slowly and in broken, halting English: "Bring the sick one. Come to my peote temple sick no more. All gone pain. Medicine heap good. Be quiet. Agent no like peote medicine. Agent doctor lose pay when medicine man make well."

Ahwaha gave him two pieces of silver and promised to tell her mother all that he had said. She had kept her promise to her mother. She had consulted the Great Medicine Man, and her doubt and distrust had increased.

This was the third day of the dance, and they expected to keep on dancing for five or six days longer. At two o'clock in the afternoon down on the river bank, beyond the settlement, the council was called, just where the ground sloped gently toward the stream and the grass was shaded by a clump of silver poplars.

A runner had gone to the homes of each one called to sit in the council, and presented a small roll of tobacco. This was a form of invitation to the Big Smoke. For an hour they sat or reclined upon the hillside and smoked in silence. Each man brought with him the little roll of tobacco presented by the runner and from these they filled their pipes. Tonto was the son of a noted Chief and accustomed to sitting in council. He came as the representative of his own tribe and Thunder Bird, who had said, "You tell me all. They only discuss. Indian can't do nothing. Agent big scare. Me tired of discuss. No good. Indian must stand by agent or go to jail."

On the hillside they smoked for an hour, then slowly and with much show of dignity, an old Indian arose and spoke only a few words in the native language. Very slowly he resumed his seat upon the ground, and they all smoked on in silence. Twenty minutes passed and then another Indian arose and answered the first speaker. Tonto did not understand all that the old men were saying, but from the interpreter he learned that the question before the council related to a good old Indian—Lone Dog—who had been allotted land some twenty years previously. Two years after said allotment the agent said to Lone Dog, "You have two children. Why not have them allotted?" "Ugh! no!" replied Lone Dog. "Law say he must be twenty-one year old and head of fam. No! no!"

Three months later the dishonest agent brought Lone Dog the allottment papers for his children, and thrust them upon him. After some parley Lone Dog, fearing the displeasure of the agent, accepted the papers. Later the agent sent a buyer from a lumbering firm to the old Indian to arrange for the purchase of the timber upon his land and that of the children.

The agent resigned. A new agent came and now Lone Dog has been notified that the land of his children would be taken from him. The transaction was illegal. Lone Dog had built his home upon the land of his children. They both had died long ago, and he had sold his personal allottment. The old Indian was now about to become homeless and penniless.

The Indians smoked their pipes, refilled them and smoked and discussed, and when at sunset Tonto and Wild Flower waved farewell to the dancers, the council was still discussing Lone Dog's misfortune, and the rascal agent who had assisted the lumber firm to unlawfully secure the timber. What could be done? Indians are not allowed to employ attorneys to represent them without permission from the commissioner of Indian affairs. Lone Dog could not read, write nor speak English, and the bad agent was gone, no one knew where. They could discuss and that was all. "Education in civil government and the English language is sorely needed by our older people," Tonto said, as the boat drifted away down stream. "Going back to the starting point with the current is play. We were a long time pulling up stream, Wild Flower, but watch the trees hurrying past us now."

The moon cast a pale, white light over the earth. The night was still and calm. Ahwaha looked away into the clouds, but she was thinking of Tonto's words. "Yes, the boat glides down stream silently and swiftly, and, Tonto, I am thinking of the Indians. They, too, are drifting down stream. No one offers any resistance. They cannot think for themselves. They can only obey or fool the agent. This whole life breeds deception. At the agency they seemed very happy, but some of them came a long distance to the dance. And what about their crops and their cattle? A dance that lasts eight and ten days must interfere with the support of the family, to say nothing of the loss of vitality and sleep. To me time and strength and intelligence are valuable. The Indians get their pittance from the government and they are carefree."

"Come away from all this, Wild Flower," Tonto pleaded, "This is not the place for you. The sky and the air and the birds and the flowers are all beautiful, but commercialism in varied forms has changed the Red Man. Come with me, Wild Flower. I cannot let you live and die here. Come, be my bride. Come, help me out in the great world, where there is thought and action."

The canoe rounded a curve in the stream. The moonlight silted through the trembling leaves and fell upon the water, and there in the shadows beneath the willows, Ahwaha saw the pale, sad face of Eugene Martel. "O, Tonto," she cried, "I know why many people believe in the return of spirits. Out from our grief and love we visualize the old scenes and the dear faces until to us the pictures are real and we believe in them. Thoughts, Tonto, are the material out of which we build our world. Tonto, I love you, you are kind and good. You understand my heart. But wait a little for my answer. I must think."

"You think of some Pale Face," Tonto cried. "Yes," replied the Indian girl, "the face I see is the face of a white man; a face from the spirit world; the face of my dear friend, Dr. Martel. But, Tonto, he was all that the Indian could be. His heart was noble and tender. His eyes saw all that was beautiful and he was loyal. Loyal to a fault. Yes, Tonto, he was loyal. He had absorbed the culture of all people, and yet he failed miserably, wretchedly, because he defied natural law. Often he said, 'I care nothing about food. I may eat if I choose or I may not eat. I may sleep or not sleep. It matters not. The mind rules.' But, Tonto, I know now that everything is governed by fixed laws, and it is our business to know the application of these laws. Dr. Martel's noble spirit could no longer dwell in such a habitation."

"What was the matter with him?" Tonto asked with a shade of impatience. "An evil spirit must have led him to use morphine. Now, I know that the real enemies are crouching in the realm of thought, ready to slay us, Tonto. Dr. Martel said, 'Until I knew you, Ahwaha, I always thought the Indians were picturesque, seen at a distance. I thought they decorated the landscape in a wild fantastic way. I had been told that they were very dangerous, and bad. But now I know that you, dear child, possess all that is best in the white race.' Tonto, the thing the whole world needs most is more truth regarding fundamentals. Knowledge would do away with segregated spots like the Indian Reservation. The Indian has the crude material, but he barters away his birthright, when he neglects the training of his intellect."

The canoe neared the bridge by Chief Thunder Bird's home. Tonto brought the little craft to land, sprang out and carefully assisted Wild Flower to gain the mossy bank that sloped abruptly up from the water. Meanwhile he said, "That is fine talk, all true, Wild Flower, but it tires the brain and makes you sick. Come with me away from this dull place where no one will, or can understand you. I am going in the morning. Come with me, Wild Flower."

She looked across the river toward the group of filthy huts she knew were nestling there among the trees. She thought of the dull, vapid, empty, aimless life of the people. To her it seemed a long, drawn-out struggle with death. "Tonto," she whispered, "I will go but not now. Come back, Tonto. I shall count the days until we meet again and I will keep on trying to help the Indians."

Tonto drew Ahwaha to him and reverently kissed her forehead. "The name is wrong," he whispered, "you are the beautiful white rose that grows in the great gardens, watched and tended with loving care. You are too frail for this place, Wild Flower. What can anyone do for the Indians in this environment? They are not as fortunate as the squirrels. Over yonder is the white man who wants to sell the Indian whiskey. Yonder is the fellow who wants the Indian's timber. Down there is one who wants to sell him bad meat, cheap tobacco, etc. Another steals fire wood from the Indian in the dead of night, and they all despise him, for his shiftless habits, dreamy moods, ignorance, and cautiousness. You must leave this place, Wild Flower, before the bad weather sets in, but teach them all you can, especially to speak English and to think. To think, Ahwaha, that is the greatest thing for any human being. The people who think cannot be enslaved."

When Wild Flower awoke on the following morning the sunlight streamed through her window and flooded the whole room. She felt lonely, for Tonto was gone and she would not see him for a long time; but she sprang up and went about the business of the day with new courage. She persuaded her mother to go outside and sit in the sunlight. "Mother, dear," she pleaded, "there is no life without sunlight, no vegetation, no growth of any sort. We cannot afford to cheat ourselves by hiding away from the sunlight. There is no life without oxygen. We cannot afford to cheat ourselves of the normal amount of fresh air, and, mother, these are absolutely free."

"Ugh! ugh!" wailed the old woman, "me see the big Medicine Man." But she was too weak to make the journey to the agency, so Chief Thunder Bird brought the Medicine Man, who prayed and cried to the Bad Spirit, "Be gone! be gone!" Over her body he made strange passes with his hands and groaned and waved a sacred crow's foot. Then he sang and administered peote buttons. This was what Mrs. Thunder Bird had been told would make her well. Accordingly, her spirits began to revive, and immediately after the administration of about the tenth button she declared, "Me better. Me sleep now."

She slept and dreamed of strange, uncanny spirits, of a long journey, of fantastic forms, and wild scenery.

Late on the following afternoon she awoke and called Ahwaha and Thunder Bird to her couch. "I am tired," she said in soft low tones, "I go to my long sleep. By and by I call you. I call all 'till you come to me. Chief Thunder Bird good, Ahwaha good child. All is good. I not afraid. The great spirit watch me." Then she straightened her body out upon the couch, closed her eyes, and lay silent and motionless until the hour preceding dawn, when her spirit departed from the lodge of the proud old chief and the gentle Wild Flower, Ahwaha.

CHAPTER IV

Starlight; Another Type of Indian Maiden

Above the blue lake lay the green hills. A path zigzagged up and down, in and out, along the wooded shore, beneath a tangled growth of shrubs and vines. At a point where the path lay close up to the bank, a small canoe glided noiselessly over the water. A tall man sat in the little craft holding the oars poised in the air. "Talk about voices," he said aloud, "that has the ring of a bird's voice; angel or bird, I must behold the owner." He rowed into a nearby cove, where the foliage was dense and the green branches dropped their points down into the blue water. Nearer came the voice, and then ceased. The man bent forward and listened for an instant only, then he parted the branches before him and was about to emerge upon the path when again he heard the refrain, "Lo! Hear the Gentle Lark!" This time still nearer. The melody rippled along spontaneous and free, like water gushing up from a spring in the hillside. The listener thought he had stumbled upon an opera singer taking her vacation beside the lake. On and on flowed the rich melody, embellished by trills and daring flights that rivaled the song of the English skylark. Then suddenly it ceased.

Cassius Mott clapped his hands vigorously, sprang from cover, and stood in the path, facing a tall, slender Indian girl. A flash of surprise passed over his face and then he cried, "Glorious! Glorious! Where did you learn to sing like that, miss? It went straight to my heart."

Starlight shrank from the handsome white man who barred her path. The red blood mounted to her cheeks and temples. She did not answer his question, but replied in low tones, "When there is music in the soul, it sings. When there is harmony in the soul, it registers sweet sounds." In her eyes there was a depth of mystery, hauteur, and suspicion. She continued, "I thought I was alone with the trees." For a moment Cassius stood abashed, then he lifted his hat, bowed low, and returned to the little canoe. He took up the oars and said aloud, "She is the daughter of an old-time Indian, by Jove. They were as proud as kings."

The boat shot out upon the water, and Cassius began to sing, "Who now will sail with me, in my bark o'er the sea?"

Starlight walked on, but she heard the white man's voice, drifting in from the lake. It rang clear and mellow. She listened for a moment, then a look of scorn passed over her face, and she, too, said aloud, "Once my people possessed all this beautiful country. They were powerful and happy, but those insolent whites drove them back, back to the barren places. Now my people starve." She clinched her fingers and went on, "But I will succeed. I will master Fate. I will have the knowledge that has made the white race great. I will conquer Fate."

That evening she sang in the big pavilion that stood on the sloping hillside above the water. Cassius Mott was there. He, too, sang, and Starlight heard the music in his voice, although she remained outwardly cold and silent. At the close of the meeting they met and were formally introduced, and Cassius said, "I knew that we two would meet again. You could not hide with such a voice. You surely will allow me to listen when you sing."

Ah, too well man knows the art of flattery. Too well he knows the heart of woman. A fascinating smile played over Starlight's face. It was a flash of the Indian girl's soul that came to the surface. To be appreciated, to be understood, to be treated kindly, was the deepest desire of her heart.

Cassius was usually surrounded by a galaxy of girls. His handsome appearance, elegant manners, and fine voice, drew all the susceptible fair ones, and brought about no end of jealousies. Starlight felt that a great gulf lay between them. She was an Indian girl, and Cassius Mott was a white man. About herself she folded her mantle of proud reserve more closely than ever, and went her solitary way.

The next day she returned to the academy in the big city where she kept her place at the head of her class, and won honors in spite of bitter jealousy. The home of Cassius chanced to be near by the school, and it was not long before he would drop in at the musical gatherings just to hear the Indian girl sing, and as the weeks passed he learned that Starlight was an exceptional student; that prejudice had sprung up among her classmates, owing to her color, and gradually his attention became centered upon the Indian girl. At first it was a sense of pity that he felt, later a form of pique. Seldom it was that any woman remained wholly indifferent to his charms, and here was an Indian girl, calm, cold, and serene in his presence. He must fathom the mystery. Starlight must be brought to his feet, and so it came about that each time she sang or recited before the academy gatherings, a page would come tripping down the aisle bearing a huge bouquet of roses, with a small white card nestling in the center, bearing the words, "To Starlight, from one who always listens—from one who hears. C. M."

By and by they met and sang together, and Cassius found the pathway to the soul of the Indian girl. Their voices mingled as one, and Starlight's dark eyes glowed and sparkled with a new light. No voice had ever before thrilled her with such perfect harmony. She had always heard an element of discord when her voice mingled with others. To sing with Cassius was harmony divine. One day when alone with Jane Condon, a classmate, she said, "Music takes me into another world, and it is hard for me to come back. It shocks my sensibilities. If I were not handicapped by birth, I would plan a career upon the operatic stage, but now I shall be a philosopher." Jane laughed aloud, "Whoever heard of a woman philosopher? You will marry, as all sensible girls do, and be content to love and be loved." Starlight shook her dark head and resolved to devote herself more and more to study and meditation. But she could not escape the attention of Cassius. He was more kind, more sympathetic, more devoted, as the days passed, until the hour came when Starlight loved him with all the depth and power within her.

One evening when they parted he placed in her hand a small pencil sketch. While she sang she had wondered what he was drawing upon the white sheet of paper. Cassius not only sang, but dabbled in law and picture-making. Starlight glanced at the scrap of paper and then hastily concealed it from prying eyes. She had looked upon a pretty cottage nestling among the trees and shrubs. A woman sat upon the veranda, holding a babe in her arms. A tall man upon the lawn among the rose bushes held by the hand a little boy. Above the picture was written, "Hark, hark the Lark," and underneath, "Our Home—my Starlight."

The Indian girl gave no outward sign, but her heart struggled to be free from restraint, from deception, from fear. Not long afterward occurred one of those strange little incidents which are really great. Cassius went with Starlight and Jane Condon for a long drive in the country. They made the start from a little suburban village. On their way back, at dusk, they were driving along quietly, when out from the shadows and clouds of dust, emerged a horse driven by a man apparently intoxicated. In an instant a struggle was on for the lead. Starlight saw the ditches upon either side. She knew that just beyond, a narrow bridge spanned a culvert. She grasped the man's arm, and for the first time spoke his name, "Cassius, Cassius, I beg of you, be careful. There is danger." Her voice trembled and her grip upon his arm was very firm. Cassius instantly reined his horse out, and brought him back upon his haunches, giving his rival the full width of the road. They saw the buggy reel and pitch from side to side, swing over the culvert, and plunge on beyond a low hill. They were rid of the dangerous horseman and then Cassius whispered, "It was worth a broken neck to hear you speak my name. Never again call me Mr. Mott."

Starlight bit her lips in shame, but it was done. Nothing could conceal the love that escaped with that one word spoken in a moment of deep anxiety. Jane began softly to sing, "Lo, Hear the Gentle Lark." "Yes, yes," said Cassius, "the Gentle Lark has an adoring audience, even at this late hour." Thus they journeyed homeward.

Starlight was happy, while the weeks and months passed. Every one at the academy predicted for her a brilliant future. Then one dark night, when the sky was heavy with low hanging clouds, Cassius came to the home of Starlight. His manner was changed. About him there was a cloak of cautious restraint. In his eyes there was an anxious troubled look. "What is it, Cassius? You are not yourself to-night," Starlight said. He sat down beside her, took her hand and spoke in that soft, winning voice that thrilled her soul. "Starlight, you are very dear to me. You possess noble qualities, far beyond those of ordinary women. No girl could claim greater respect. I really must explain myself to-night. I have had a very pleasant dream, but to-day I awakened to the truth. My family, you know, are very proud. They have some grand old ancestors—and—well—to-day they came to see me—two of my most distinguished relatives, and, Starlight, they are shocked by my conduct—by my attention to you. I have viewed the subject from various angles and I guess they are right. I have arrived at the conclusion that it would be an injustice for me to marry outside of my circle."

The dark eyes of the Indian girl contracted. Her face took on an ashen tinge. She did not speak, nor look toward the man who had thus stabbed her. She silently glided from the room, closed the door very gently, while she walked as one asleep. The curtain had been lowered upon their love scene. Cassius waited a long time for the return of the Indian girl, and then he hurried out into the night, muttering, "A bit of unpleasant business, but, by Jove, I came through with flying colors."

Through the long hours of that horrible night Starlight battled with her grief and humiliation. When the morning dawned she looked into her little mirror and beheld a haggard, ugly face. She lifted her clinched hand and shook it at the Indian girl before her. "I hate the Pale Face," she said aloud. "Death is in my soul, but I will live. I will not soil my hands, and I will not be crushed. I will triumph over every obstacle. I will forget and I will help to redeem my race. He knew when first he looked upon my face that I was an Indian. I did not deceive him. A long time he was finding out that he was too good to marry an Indian girl. I was indifferent. He saw my indifference and compelled me to love him. Now he compels me to hate him. He will never know that the heart of the Indian bleeds. I can live without love. I will master Fate. Murder is in my heart but I will not soil my hands upon him. No, Starlight will live without revenge."

The days dragged on. At night Starlight's eyes were red with weeping, but when she stepped from the solitude of her own little room, all the calm stoicism, all the caution and deception of the Indian was wrapped about her. From the academy she was graduated with highest honors. She did not deign to speak with members of her class. She stood apart, cold, proud, silent, while all the time in the depths of her great dark eyes a fire burned. A messenger came, bearing an armful of flowers from the man she now hated. She pointed to the floor. He laid them down and Starlight pushed them from her with her foot.

This terrible grief and chagrin soon did its work and Starlight was ill. Her plans for the future had been carefully laid, but suddenly she had been deprived of the power to execute them. "They shall not know that I am ill. He would understand," she muttered. On the morrow she disappeared, without one word of explanation. No one knew where or why.

CHAPTER V

Tonto as Scout

"Just the man I'm looking for!" Dr. Nachito grasped Tonto's hand and pulled him through the doorway. "Come in. Come in. Where have you been? When did you reach the city? Say, Tonto, where is Starlight?"

No, Tonto did not know. And Dr. Nachito settled back in his great arm chair. A grave, earnest look came into his eyes. "Tonto, I must find her. I have written and my letter was returned. I have no time, understand, to trace her. Help me find the girl, Tonto. Strange that she disappeared in that way. She had been offered a position at Carlisle. But at the close of her school year she just dropped out of sight. I believe that Starlight is teaching on one of the Western reservations, probably some distance from her own tribe. She feels very bitter toward certain white people and she hates notoriety, understand. Starlight is a wonderful girl, but too shy. I expect great things of her. She represents the high-minded, lofty-souled Indian woman. Her intelligence ranks with the best. No white woman ever possessed more native ability. I am proud of Starlight, understand. Tonto, how long before you go West?"

"I dropped in, doctor, to say good-by. I go to-morrow. If Starlight is out there, I will find her. She cannot hide that voice."

"No, no," the doctor replied, with a hearty laugh, "she sings just like the birds, understand. It is easier for them to sing than to keep still. That's what I call music."

For an hour Tonto lounged upon the big davenport, while they discussed matters pertaining to their race, and when they parted the doctor said, "Tell Starlight to come, or communicate with me, and, Tonto, show the whites that we are men—that we belong to the great human family—and don't forget to come back. Tonto, there is a chair and the davenport and a pillow always waiting for you. My people are always welcome, and the friends of my people. It is a real pleasure to greet them here and share what I have. Farewell, Tonto, and don't forget to come back."

CHAPTER VI

The Trail

On a midsummer evening Tonto sat on the ground before a camp-fire, in company with a dozen Indian friends. A chilly wind swept down from the north and they drew close to the little fire, smoked their pipes and discussed famous hunting expeditions. The fire burned low and then Tonto began to sing. The Indians listened in silence. He finished his song and then one young lad sat up very straight and said, "Up stream three miles a girl lives with friends. She teach school in winter—she sing fine, fine. Her name Starlight." Tonto bounded to his feet, "Where? Which way? Tell me. I know Starlight." When the boy had imparted all the information he possessed Tonto whistled in imitation of the night birds and danced the Happy Dance about the smoking fire. He had given up all hope of finding Starlight long ago, and here he stumbled upon her trail at the last moment, for to-morrow he would turn back toward the great metropolis. Round the fire Tonto executed the Ghost Dance, the War Dance, the Peace Dance, the Medicine Dance, all in one. If only the boy had told him earlier in the evening. It was now midnight, and he must wait until morning.

But before sunrise he was up and impatient to start in search of Starlight. He took the sleepy Indian boy with him—the boy who had heard Starlight sing. It seemed a short three miles, and when they reached the small circle of huts upon the bank of the river, no one was stirring. "Come along, lad," he commanded, "we will take the first canoe we find and row about until the Indians come outside." They trudged along for a few rods, when suddenly Tonto heard the voice of Starlight. "Hark, hark, the lark at Heaven's gate sings." The tones rang out clear, and for a moment Tonto was unable to speak or stir. The pink and gold of morning gilded all the hills and tree tops, and the voices of a thousand birds seemed blended with the matin song of the Indian girl. "That is Starlight. That is Starlight," Tonto whispered, "dear child of Nature," and then he bounded down the path and came upon the Indian girl sitting on a boulder that hung out over the water. Her bare head and arms and feet were bathed in a flood of sunlight. Tonto touched the brim of his straw hat and laughed aloud, when Starlight sprang from the rock and greeted him. "That was mighty rude to cut short a song like that, Starlight, but I must be gone and I have a message for you to deliver from Dr. Nachita. He is very anxious regarding you, anxious to see you, Starlight. He insisted upon my finding you. He wants you to return to the city."

An expression of contempt swept over the girl's face and then she smiled, "The doctor is a good friend to all Indians. Tonto, I think that I will go. I cannot remain here. Reservation life is intolerable. The Indians distrust those who have been among the whites. They build a wall about themselves and leave you outside. I cannot go back to the old way of living. The agent dislikes educated Indians. He makes you feel unwelcome. I have decided to live with the white race and work for the Indian. I hate the Pale Face, Tonto, but I must have knowledge and culture. I cannot exist in this aimless, lifeless way." "The advice of Dr. Nachita will be valuable to you, Starlight. He has lived the life of the white man for forty years. He has attended their schools, dwelt in their homes. He has the white man's education and the Indian's heart. He stands between the two races. Go to him, Starlight."

The Indian girl promised to see the doctor or to communicate with him in the near future. When they parted upon the river bank, Starlight cried out, "Hear the birds, Tonto. See how the sunlight bathes the whole earth. But the people! Something has gone wrong with them."

CHAPTER VII

Memories

Dr. Nachita was writing big, terse sentences between spells of pounding the table. "The Indian is a man like other men," he wrote, "and the Indian will come up faster than any other race when given a chance."

The door opened and Starlight stepped inside. She did not speak but smiled just a wee bit. Dr. Nachita lifted his head and then bounded from his chair, and upset the inkwell upon the Navajo spread. "Why, child," he roared, "where have you been all this time? Why did you run away? Nonsense! Nonsense! You might have had a fine position at Carlisle."

The girl replied in not over-confident tones, "I was ill. I could no longer endure being stared at by white people. I went back to the Indians that I might escape notice, and rest. I was tired, tired. But, doctor, the reservation is no place for educated Indians. I would go mad if unable to escape from the dull, monotonous, restricted, aimless life they lead, with no incentive, no hope, no aim."

"Yes! Yes! I understand. I know it is awful; no place for you, Starlight; a waste of time; but we must master Fate! Fate, you understand, is simply environment and circumstances. Starlight, we must master Fate!"

He closed his eyes and shook his great shaggy black head. Presently he arose and shook his fist at the girl:

"You ran away from a common mongrel cur. You! A noble Indian girl! You hated and hate made you ill. You should be teaching at Carlisle; you wasted a lot of perfectly good energy, power, understand, that we need. A great responsibility rests upon our few educated Indians. We are to lead the whole race. Sit down there while I tell you a sad story." Starlight obeyed. The doctor went back to his chair, closed his eyes, and began to speak in tones so low that Starlight leaned forward to catch the sounds. "Starlight, I was called to the bedside of a dying woman, the mother of a babe. To me she said, 'Doctor, where is the Indian girl they call Starlight? Tell her that I did not steal from her the white man.' 'Whom do you have reference to?' I questioned. 'Did you never hear of Cassius Mott, the white man who rejected Starlight because she was an Indian?' 'Well! well!' I replied, 'I am glad to know that Starlight escaped such a man.' 'Well,' she continued, 'I met him after he had lost sight of Starlight.' 'That was good,' I remarked. 'There was no more Starlight for him; go on.' 'He never mentioned the Indian girl to me until we were married. Then he bragged about his irresistible charms for women. I compelled Mott to marry me,' she went on hurriedly, 'he did not intend to take a wife, but I taught him a lesson. He left me with the baby there.' She nodded toward an infant sleeping in the corner of the room. 'Now I am dying. Who will care for my child? Cassius Mott was never in love with anyone but himself. He was handsome, and this was his ruin.' 'Where is the cur?' I asked. 'Gone to the dogs,' she continued, 'in jail for forgery. He is a physical wreck. Cassius Mott's star has set. I know from the lips of Mott that Starlight went back to reservation life to hide her grief. I fear she holds me responsible; but, doctor, I did not meet Mott until after Starlight had disappeared; and would to God that I had never known him; all he possessed was good looks and egotism.'

"Well, Starlight, the woman died that night. Her last words were, 'Ask Starlight to love my child. The father said, "Starlight is noble and loyal, but she is an Indian."' "

Starlight looked aghast. She did not speak, but shrank back into the corner of the big davenport. In her face Dr. Nachita read the answer—"Foster the child of Cassius Mott? Never!"

"There! There! Starlight," the doctor pleaded, "just think about it. Just think very calmly, very sensibly, and by and by give me your answer. Resentment and grief have made you sick. Sickness makes you weak and helpless. Passion is destructive. Time is precious. You have the elements of greatness. Use those forces, Starlight, for the glory of our race. Think of this little motherless, helpless baby. What has he done that we should not love him? He has wronged no one. Carry out the mother's wish, Starlight. It will prove an anchor for your soul. It is not the object of our love, but the love itself that saves us, understand—it is the love itself that transforms the life."

At last Starlight replied, "And you ask me to adopt the child of that man, Dr. Nachita? Why?"

"The helplessness and dependence, and innocence, of the child will save you, Starlight, from hate and bitterness. When our heads and hearts and hands are full of work, there is no time for hate and bitterness. This is the lesson our race must learn. We who think and reason must lead the way; would to God that I had gotten the light long years ago. Do not go back to your people, sitting in darkness, Starlight. Stay here where conditions are more helpful, where it is no crime to think, understand. Forget yourself and all the past. Sorrow and pain do not hang around long when we ignore them. Let us teach our people to forget, and then, Starlight, the pale face will forget those things which you and I do not care to remember in the history of our race. Dear child, we must forget. It was a horrid misunderstanding, but, Starlight, had our race bent all their energy toward finding the way to live peaceably with the pale face, instead of nursing hate and revenge, there would be no great gulf between us."

The Indian girl glared at him and opened her lips, but the doctor continued, "There! There! I must forget. I must not regret or reprove. I must go forward. I must deal with the present. I must be the bridge over which my people pass to something better. The child is the present. He demands attention. I must go now. Think about it, Starlight. Wait here for me or come back. The door is always open."

The doctor had been gone a long time and still Starlight sat crouching in the corner of the big davenport, that was completely concealed by Navajo blankets of unique design and weave. The girl was battling with the dead past, fighting the phantoms of yesterdays. She was pitying the woman Starlight; when, in reality, Fate had been kind; she had escaped; she was free; the other woman was dead. The room was filled with brown and purple shadows, when suddenly that phantom chaser, the sunlight, came streaming through a window. It fell upon the table where here and there lay scraps of paper upon which the doctor had written down in a bold hand, his latest thoughts regarding the future of his race. It fell across the Navajo blanket; it illumined the whole room; it warmed the hands of the Indian girl; it gilded her jet black hair and heightened the color in her cheeks. A new light came into her eyes and a smile transformed her whole countenance. She blinked as one just awakened from sound sleep. She arose, drew her cape about her shoulders and passed out as silently as she had entered.

CHAPTER VIII

The Wild Flower Fades

When Tonto arrived at the lodge of Chief Thunder Bird, he found Ahwaha lying ill, upon a pile of blankets, under a small white tepee which the old chief had placed upon the green bank above the river. She was looking away into the blue sky, through drifts of fleecy white clouds, when Tonto appeared in the opening. "Ahwaha, dear child, what has happened?" She cried out, "O, Tonto, I feared you would not come in time." Her voice was like the voice of a child after much suffering. She held up her hands toward the great strong man who bent over her tenderly. Tonto knelt down and lifted Ahwaha and placed her head against his breast. "Child, I came to take you away from this dreary place. I have money now. I sold the land my father left me. Ahwaha, you must be brave—you must live! We will go to-morrow if you wish." He spoke hurriedly and great tears trembled on his eyelids.

"Sit there, Tonto, by the door. I smother. I am tired—always. I will speak slowly. I must tell you, Tonto," she whispered, "I am going away, going to meet mother and my one dear friend. Tonto, my heart is broken. I cannot endure the life here. The misery and hopelessness of the people have eaten deep into my heart. I have tried to help, but, Tonto, effort is useless. The reservation system is wrong; it saps the life and ambition. There is nothing to look forward to, nothing to inspire hope or effort. Black ignorance is the natural atmosphere. When mother left us, my father thought he must abandon the home where death had entered. I could not give up all for which I had labored so strenuously. Poverty is one of the afflictions of our race. They must learn to cling to their possessions. I would not give up the home, so father went alone to the agency. He returned when friends informed him that I was very ill. Aunt Lizzie Waco, the good soul, has been a mother to me.

"You remember the first hut at the edge of the clearing, where the old-fashioned flowers bloomed along the path and under the windows? I gave the flowers to Aunt Lizzie and assisted her in paying for a little cottage-organ, because Aunt Lizzie sings. She loves to sing, and together we have passed many hours singing the old familiar songs. The one she loves best is, 'Where the River Shannon Flows.' Tonto, the Indians have souls. There is no gift possessed by the white man which is not theirs if only their environment were favorable to its development. My heart bleeds for them, Tonto."

The man's eyes were blinded by tears; he could not speak. Ahwaha continued, "Something terrible happened here, Tonto—a scandal regarding the agent. The circumstance was so openly immoral, I could not remain quiet. I drew up a petition asking for his removal. All the Indian men who can write signed their names to the paper. I signed for those who cannot write, and then I made a copy and mailed it to Washington. And, Tonto, I received a letter of reprimand from the commissioner and was branded a forger. The commissioner came with the agent and talked in a threatening and insulting manner. He would not examine the original petition with the names signed by all Indians at this point who can write, although I offered the petition in evidence. Maybe I did wrong; but, Tonto, the trouble involved a young Indian girl. I thought I had a right to act in her defense. O, Tonto, I am so tired! I have tried—I have tried to help them! Promise, Tonto, that when I am dead you will not let my body rest on the river bank where the others are with the little board sheds over them and all manner of trinkets inside. Come close, Tonto."

He knelt beside her and Ahwaha whispered, "Tonto, I can die content if you promise that my ashes shall be placed in the grave with the ashes of Dr. Martel. In my little black trunk you will find a letter directing you to his grave."

"It shall be so," Tonto whispered.

She fell back upon the rude couch and lay with closed eyes. Tonto bowed his head and kissed her pale lips. Then he sprang to his feet. The tent was filled with shadows, for the sun had gone down behind the silver poplars. He beckoned to the old chief who sat alone upon the river bank, dreaming the old sad dreams.

Thunder Bird crept into the tent. He laid his hand very gently upon Ahwaha's raven locks. He looked upon her pale face, and then he sank upon the ground and wailed and moaned:

"The Little Lark is dead! The Great Spirit is angry with me! Why did I not get the great Medicine Man? It was wrong for the little one to go away to school and to the big town, and come back with such notions in her pretty head. She used to sing and I forgot to hate the whites. I was no more angry. But now for two moons she no sing. She say something won't let her breathe—something make her too sad. She can no sing. She want to go to her doctor and he now live with God. I will follow. I cannot live here. Now I will burn the house."

He drew from his pocket a knife, bared his breast and slashed it; and then cut off his hair close to his head. Tonto laid his hand upon the arm of Thunder Bird and said:

"Listen, chief, to the teaching of Ahwaha, your own beautiful daughter. There was more real wisdom in her way of thinking than the people understood. She said, 'Tonto, the earth has too many people; they are crowding each other; the Indians must settle down and remain in one spot and hold fast to their property; the ground is in demand; in order to live, people must concentrate their forces; make good use of the intellect, the strength, and the time—these are the forces that make for success.' "

"What do we care about all that?" sobbed Thunder Bird. "Ahwaha is dead. I no understan what you say. The Lark no more sing."

Tonto turned away, shook his head, and muttered:

"It is this accursed reservation system that fosters and nourishes their poverty and ignorance; but I can do nothing. I will keep my promise to the Wild Flower and go my way. No more Indian life for me."

The lamentations for the dead girl were kept up all through the night, and participated in by all the Indians of that section of the reservation. Tonto was grave and silent. He had learned that grief does not demand a noisy manifestation. Tonto was troubled; how could he remove the body of Ahwaha? There was the agent, always watching, lynx-eyed. It would be useless to ask permission; the agent preferred having the old traditions carried on; it perpetuated the sort of Indians which made the bureau system necessary. At last Tonto decided upon a plan. He kept his own counsel. After the body of Ahwaha had been laid in the ground, he took from beside the door where she had placed it, a large white rose-bush and planted it at the head of her grave to mark the spot. Tonto gave money to Chief Thunder Bird and Aunt Lizzie. The old chief could not be induced to re-enter the house. When all was over he said, "No, Tonto, I go with the Medicine Man back to the agency."

When Tonto boarded the train that carried him from the village he had signed a compact with two nondescript white men whereby, for a money consideration, they were to deliver the body of Ahwaha at the depot of a railway junction fifty miles down the line. They were to go at night, "and mind that you make no mistake in the grave."

Tonto said. "Find the tall rosebush; I tied a white ribbon to one stalk low down; the name Ahwaha is on the ribbon; bring that piece of ribbon but do not disturb the rose-bush."

He could trust these henchmen, for both had grievances against the Indian agent.

A week passed before Tonto reached the city with the body and succeeded in making out the papers and having the body incinerated, and then he went on a very dark night, alone, carrying the little receptacle which contained the ashes of Ahwaha, to the grave of Dr. Martel, carefully removed a square of sod near the head of the grave and hid the little box in the earth. He kissed the bit of ribbon and placed it under the metal box, replaced the piece of sod, and murmured:

"I have kept my vow to the noblest, sweetest soul that ever came to this sad world. Farewell, Ahwaha—Wild Flower—the Lark! The Indian's word is sacred."

Then Tonto scaled the high fence for the second time and disappeared in deep shadows.

CHAPTER IX

A Decision

Dr. Nachita looked up from his writing and there in the doorway stood Starlight. "Well! Well! I knew you would come back! Good girl! Looking fine! Sit there!" He pointed to the corner of the davenport and Starlight sat down upon the Navajo blanket and leaned against a yellow satin cushion. "News for you, Starlight," he continued, "the father is dead. The child is not well—needs care, you understand." While he talked Starlight looked away into space. After a time she said, "Where is the child, doctor? I came for the baby. It has taken me all this time to find employment and establish a little home."

"My! My! Starlight, I am proud of you; depend upon me; I will help when help is needed, understand? Wait! Wait!" He left the room and returned, carrying an infant in his arms. "Understand, Starlight, I do not advise the adoption of the child; but it must have immediate care."

Starlight took the babe in her arms, and the little fellow looked up and smiled. The compact was sealed. "It was the dying woman's request, Starlight, the last words spoken by the mother; she had confidence in you founded upon the father's respect." Again Dr. Nachita left the room. This time he returned bearing a small package—"All that belongs to the child," he said, "All Indian women are good mothers; keep up the tradition, Starlight. There is a lot of bosh and nonsense about not being able to love another's child like your own. The world has too many people now. It is far more noble to care for some homeless waif who is here without being consulted, who is helpless and homeless—far more noble, understand, than to bring more children into the world. The human heart is capable of great love, great devotion, great sacrifice. This love and devotion saves us from our own miserable selves. Understand, Starlight, it is the love that saves. Shall I go with you and help you with the youngster?"

"No," Starlight replied, "outside the woman waits who will live with me and care for the child. I must furnish the support." "Yes! Yes! I understand," the doctor continued in a dreamy mood, "women are wonderful planners—far more resourceful than men. This other woman—who is she?" "A woman who has lost her only child and her husband. She has no home. She is willing to work." "There! There! See how it works out. Already matters are adjusting themselves."

The two women left with the infant. The Indian woman was young and beautiful but not overly strong in appearance. The white woman was of middle age, pale and thin, of the wiry type, born for endurance. The door closed and Dr. Nachita sat dreaming before a pile of unanswered letters. "What was it about that youngster?" he whispered, "that wrung my heart? One time I suppose that I was quite as helpless." He closed his eyes and by and by the tears fell from beneath their lids. "The Indian mothers love their children. My mother! God only knows her sorrow. I am going back. My sisters! What of them? I am going back! My childhood rises up before me like a terrible nightmare. I must know the truth. I must search for proof regarding their fate. I have taken all the comforts and blessings, and fortune has been very kind to me. But what of them? A man cannot forget his mother. The relation is too close. This poor little fellow awakens memories, strange memories in me, that have lain dormant for many years. I cannot shake them off. Starlight will be faithful. She will, I am sure. Now I am going back to that rock-ribbed, sun-parched region where most growing things bear spikes and needles for protection. I am going to hunt for my people."

CHAPTER X

The Miracle

The soul of Tonto was saturated with gloom. He had lost the comradeship and affection of a noble woman. The beauty and fragrance of the Wild Flower were only memories now. He was more lonely than ever before in his whole life. He must shake off the sad thoughts that clung to him. With this tender, sacred memory hidden deep in the recesses of his being, he walked into a big play-house on a broad thoroughfare, where the lights dazzled and bewildered him. The play was "Othello." He entered late and the scene before him presented the Moor in the presence of Brabantio and his beautiful daughter relating his adventures. The scene might have been one from "East Lynne" or "Uncle Tom's Cabin," so far as concerned Tonto. But who is this glorious Desdemona? Tonto could not turn his eyes away from her. He never had looked upon a creature of such strange fascinating beauty. He trembled and shrank from the vision before him. He grasped the arms of his chair. He must be calm; the Indian was a Stoic; Tonto Cabo had traditions to uphold. He would take root and grow fast to the chair, but expose his thoughts or emotions—never! Was he in sympathy with the gentle suffering Desdemona? Why, Tonto was anxious to leap down upon the stage, exterminate the entire company and rescue Desdemona. All the Indian bravery long pent up was now aroused. Tonto, the calm, quiet, stoical Indian, awakened as from a dream. When the curtain descended upon the last scene, he pulled himself together and walked away. Not the same Tonto! Not into the same world! A miracle had taken place! Everything seemed changed.

He read from the program the following: "Chiquita, the Spanish actress, plays Desdemona as few have played the great role. She ranks with the greatest. Her gentle pathos is irresistible. She is ravishingly beautiful and possesses the dramatic and emotional temperament. Chiquita is very young and we predict a brilliant future for this child of the gods. She has the dark, rich, glowing beauty of the Latin type. Her hair is black as the raven's wing and frames a face of wonderful plasticity, a mirror of the emotions from which shine eyes whose midnight depths at one moment seem fathomless wells of tenderness, and at another unquenchable volcanoes of blazing wrath; eyes that the love-light makes surprisingly feminine, which anger and rage make terrible."

And those were the eyes that had set the soul of Tonto on fire. He crushed the little program between his strong fingers and shoved it down into his pocket. He joined the throng that surged along the street and wandered aimlessly about, struggling with his new problem. Suddenly he muttered, "Great Caesar! The ticket! Only one more performance. What if they were sold out?" He turned about and moved through the crowds with that manner peculiar to people who know where they are going. Arrived at the box office, he secured one of the last tickets sold. for Chiquita's farewell appearance. The seat was located close to the stage, and Tonto took possession of it long before the curtain was raised. Near the close of the performance Chiquita asked, "Who is the copper-colored, big, handsome fellow close down in front?" Someone peered out from behind the scenes and pronounced him, "An Indian," and Chiquita went to her dressing-room, thinking Tonto a rich East Indian merchant or diplomat. Once her great luminous eyes rested upon the face of Tonto for a moment, and a smile rippled away from her lips; a smile that sent Tonto away happy. But how could he approach this wonderful being? Would it be possible to speak with her? After all, he thought, perhaps she only smiled at the peculiar color of his skin? Tonto kept on with his dreams and schemes until near dawn of the following day. But, he was standing by the window of the ticket office of the theater when the agent arrived next day. Tonto asked, "Where has Chiquita gone?" A strange feeling of giddiness and suffocation seized him when the man named a city five hundred miles away. "They are booked for a week there." One week! He must not lose the trail. He prepared to leave town on the first train that would carry him in that direction. Then he hurried to the home of Dr. Nachita.

"Yes! Yes! Starlight came back; wonderful woman; great prospects; not another like Starlight. Tonto, remember that we few educated Indians have a great work before us. We must teach the whole human race the truth regarding the Indian people. They must be made to understand that we are not different from other men, only those on the reservations lack the proper environment."

Tonto listened in silence. On other occasions when they met the doctor's philosophy had sounded intelligent and interesting—a real possibility for his people—but now! every consideration had dwindled into utter nothingness in the presence of his one thought—Chiquita—and so he hurried away from his Indian friend, on to the distant city. When he reached his destination he never once stopped until he had located the theater and secured a season ticket. Luckily, Tonto had sold his land on the last trip West. He was rich so long as the money lasted. Every night Chiquita looked across the footlights and beheld Tonto sitting erect and calm, and she knew that he devoured each sound that fell from her lips and was happy when she smiled, and miserable when she pretended misery. As the evenings passed Tonto more and more adored the fascinating Chiquita. When the company traveled, Tonto also traveled. From city to city the tall, handsome Indian patiently followed the star of his destiny. One evening a well-known Indian attorney accompanied him to theater. "How can I compel Chiquita to speak with me?" Tonto whispered. His friend replied, "After the play we will go behind the scenes. I have had business with the stage manager—have known him a long time."

Could it be that Tonto heard aright? Was it possible that his friend could bring about a meeting? "Lawyers are mighty smart fellows—leave it to them," Tonto whispered, and then he fell to getting command of himself, for he felt giddy and wished himself out on a reservation where he could stretch himself out once and empty his lungs.

From that night Tonto had actual faith in the ability of the Indian, especially the Indian lawyer; for he actually stood face to face with Chiquita, when the stage performance was over, and she smiled at Tonto just as she had in the play, although he was conscious that pride and hauteur looked out from her flashing eyes. Only a few words—senseless words—were spoken; but when they parted she lifted a beautiful, shapely, white hand and Tonto raised it to his lips. Chiquita's eyes swept over the handsome, tall, lithe form before her, she shook the mass of inky ringlets that tumbled about her face, and darted away to her dressing room. Tonto stammered, "I hope that we meet again." "O, yes," she laughed and looked back over her shoulder, "you will be down there, close to the stage, and I shall always see you."

And Tonto was there, watching Chiquita with great jealous eyes. To him it promised certain life or death. He scarcely knew the name of the play; the plot had no meaning for him; it was just Chiquita, the most adorable, most perfect, most gifted creature on earth.

Back across the continent flitted Chiquita with Tonto close upon her trail. One night the stage manager snarled, "I am tired of that big Indian about the stage entrance." In that hour fate also turned her back upon Chiquita, the petted, adored, spoiled child of the gods. Suddenly they all began to hurry past Chiquita, with cold, blank faces. When she questioned they all were ill—suffering from grip—had bad news—worried with business or debts, etc. And Chiquita was driven to accept the love and sympathy of Tonto—big, handsome Tonto with the soft, musical voice, who sang Indian love songs, and love songs that were not Indian, and pleaded, "Chiquita, be my bride and I will defy the world; I could not love you more; let us wed."

And Chiquita at last cast her fate with that of the Indian, Tonto Cabo. Just why she never was able to explain to her own satisfaction. Other handsome men—wealthy barons and gifted actors had sought her hand in marriage and showered upon her love and adoration. Tonto offered nothing but his heart, and one golden morning, when the earth was bathed in sunlight they went to a quiet little parsonage in the suburbs and were married.

The show season closed and Chiquita was dropped from the company's pay-roll. She had married an Indian. The men of the company felt belittled. The great actor refused to appear with the wife of an Indian. Chiquita was defiant. She stormed and berated their lack of appreciation for real art. Proud and sure of her marvelous gifts, she flouted criticism. Tonto had money from the sale of his land—she would have her own company. She could write her own plays. She would trample upon defeat. For the present she would rest in some far-away sylvan retreat where, unobserved, she could worship the beauty and grandeur of nature. They purchased a birch-bark canoe—moccasins—leggins—guns—a tent—and other necessary equipment for a long vacation in the forest and upon the water. With these they journeyed to a little green island in one of the Great Lakes, where Chiquita was queen of the Isle and Tonto was Chief Great Eagle.

Undisturbed save by an occasional swift thunderstorm, they dreamed away the long summer days. For Tonto it was the Indian life of song and story. For Chiquita, it stilled a call from the wild, a sort of revolutionary instinct within her that always cried out against restraint. She sang and danced, she imitated the birds, she chased the wild animals, and ruthlessly tore from their stalks great armfuls of wild flowers, with which she decorated the tepee and made wreaths to adorn the brow of Chief Great Eagle. Then she grew tired of the solitude and pouted; and finally shipped the whole paraphernalia to Dr. Nachita, Tonto's friend, and rushed back to the big city.

CHAPTER XI

Old Memories Awakened

Where morning guilds the hilltops fair;
And songs of birds make glad the air;
Where rock and stream reflect the light;
Where flowers unfold their colors bright;
There I would rest, there I would dream;
In forest dark and valley green.

A strange man who could not speak their language had appeared in their midst. "What means this?" growled Chief Ugly Bear. "He sure belong to us; he tell he has lived with pale face many year; he come back and say—'know you a little boy stolen long years ago, sold to pale face? I am that child; my name is Wawa.' He say, 'Tell me of my mother—of my family—all. I recall one awful night; the big camp-fire burn up high; fierce black fellows came yelling like mad and storm our camp; they shout and club and capture all; big Indian take me on his horse; we ride all night; then tall good white man give Indian money and take me away.' He say, 'Pale face good; but my sisters—what of them? My mother and father—what of them? I come to know by you.' "

Ugly Bear closed his eyes and lapsed into silence. By and by he straightened himself up and said, "This is the child of Singing Bird; it must be so. The father was killed in that raid and she be separated from children. She hear that little boy be in hostile camp. She run like hunted deer over the stony places and cry 'Wawa! Wawa!' The Indian scout he go after Singing Bird to bring back to agency. She no stop when he call 'Halt!' She plunge on into canyon. Scout he shoot and there lay Singing Bird dead on rocks. We no more hear 'bout little boy. Now he come back fine Indian. Send out runners; call my people; we dance long time; tell squaws bake mescal. Tell all to bring presents, the child of Singing Bird found. We go to God's tent and offer peote. The Great Spirit smile."

And so at sunset one golden day the Indians gathered in the valley about the lodge of Chief Ugly Bear. They came softly, for it was the moment of silence preceding the disappearance of the crimson sun behind the mountains, when there is no sound of wild life. They lighted a camp-fire and spread beautiful blankets upon the ground before the child of Singing Bird; upon the blankets they laid their gifts of pottery and woven ware. There were baskets over which their women had labored many weary days, and into which they had woven the traditions of a race; designs passed down from mother to daughter, through endless generations. Wawa bowed his head and wept; he could not speak; no words came to his lips; but what of words at such moments? They jar and confuse.

About the camp-fire they danced and sang and feasted upon the mescal that had baked three days in the earth-oven. While from the desert came the howling of the coyotes, their weird voices rising and falling upon the night wind, until the midnight hour. Far into the night it was when Wawa lay down upon a blanket beneath the deep dark sky. He listened for the cry of the coyote, but they had gone to rest. Then he looked into the dark heavens and watched the great stars creep along their paths.

"My! My! They are big and bright and so near," he murmured, "God is surely watching over us. Justice comes slowly, because not all people think. I will wait. I will not hate. How can I hate with such a world of beauty and mystery about me?" Then he fell asleep as the child Wawa.

The dancing continued and the muffled sounds from the tom-tom rolled down the valley among the black shadows. Just before dawn Wawa awakened; he heard sweet sounds;

someone was singing; he raised himself and sat upon the ground and listened. He thought the voice was that of a young girl. The melody rose higher and higher, then fell in soft, mournful cadences. Up through the darkness it soared again and again, trembling with pathos, then died out and silence reigned. "An angel! An angel!" whispered Wawa. Something was struggling up from the shadows of the past. Slowly he raised his hands and held them up toward the dark sky. "My mother! My mother! That is a song she sang; from out the dim past it comes back to me."

He bowed his head and listened eagerly, but only the voices of the mourning doves came to his ears. They were cooing to their mates, calling back and forth, and then all sounds were hushed and Wawa wept and waited, while the sun shot up through a bank of gray that hung low in the east, and the whole earth was flooded with bright, golden light, for day had dawned.

When the camp was astir he inquired of the interpreter, "Who was singing in the night? I never heard such music.. I thought the Indians had no music. That was divine!" The Indian answered, "That was my mother singing; she not often sing like that; all the camp keep still and listen." "I cry and wish she sing more," Wawa continued. "That sweet voice, throbbing through the darkness, trembling with pathos, brought back my childhood and I felt the presence of my mother, but I thought the voice that of a girl. You tell me each singer uses his own words—improvises to suit the melody and the occasion? What a pity, what a shame, the Indians keep no records. Lost! Yes, I tell you everything my people once possessed is lost."

The stranger was no longer the child Wawa, but Dr. Nachita, protesting bitterly against the fate of his race.

Late in the day little groups of Indians came to discuss land, and treaty, and annuity problems. Through the interpreter the doctor learned many things regarding the dull, aimless life they led, and the utter lack of hope and initiative among those living upon reservations.

"There must be a change. Just how it will come about I cannot say, understand, but I will not rest until something is done to stop this retrograde movement of my people. But, my! my! who comes here? Such grace and beauty! Just like a young fawn! The white women should see this pretty creature. Envious? I should say."

A young Indian girl approached and sat down quite close to him. He continued the conversation with the interpreter and looked very grave, with his eyes turned toward the canyon. "I must not frighten the pretty child; she would run like the wild deer that she is. Well! Well! I never saw one so beautiful. The sunset colors tint her olive skin and jet black hair. How wonderful! Her brown bare ankles and the beads and bracelets, and that pretty figured dress; 'short sleeves and low neck,' the ladies call it. My. but I wish they could see her! They would go mad with jealousy. My, if I could only paint pictures on canvas! O, yes, I have the picture in my head, but say, that girl is marvelous." At that moment she looked up into the grave face of Dr. Nachita, as a young deer might look upon a strange creature in repose. Her large, black eyes glinted and sparkled like dew drops in the bright sunlight.

The doctor spoke to "the child," as he called her, and in his heart he thanked Heaven that he was a bachelor. He smiled upon the whole family, for the mother and father were close at hand, and for the moment he forgot to upbraid the pale face.

Months afterward a reporter asked, "Have you ever loved an Indian woman, doctor?" "Well, no, but last summer I thought I was in love with a very young Indian girl —only fifteen, understand. My! my! but she was beautiful! Hers was just natural, simple, unconscious beauty, and I always associate a fawn with my memory of the child. I wrote to her after reaching the city, possibly twice, and finally a letter came from the mamma, a very crude, clumsy affair, but indicating that I might have the girl, understand; but in the meantime, I had pondered over the matter and decided that the little beauty would be compelled to surrender too much. In the city she could not run bare-headed, bare-footed, and bare-armed. That magnificent black hair could not tumble about her shoulders and frame her pretty face. She could not romp along the river and climb the rocky trails; and she would pine for the wild life and weep her eyes out, and I would be miserable, too, and wish her back with her mamma and curse the day that I disturbed their simple pastoral life. But, understand, I carry the picture in my memory and I know that is best. No one can step directly from that life into this world in which we live, without being disturbed by the change. She was beautiful, and her voice! I hear it now—very low and sweet, and her manner so natural and artless and reposeful. I saw her only three times, always accompanied by the mother. The last time she sat nearby and while I talked she interpreted for me. As I smiled upon her she looked down toward her bare brown feet, drew her skirts about her, arose and stepped aside, without making a sound. I looked down and saw a snake gliding past her, a long, dangerous-looking fellow. We all jumped to our feet, and almost instantly an Indian dispatched the enemy with a club. The interpreter said, 'A bad omen, doctor—that meant the pale face who came between.'"

CHAPTER XII

The End of the Trail

They both paced the station platform; both looked toward the mountains and then into the blue sky beyond. Both had the look of dreamers; the Indian and the white man "glorious country; wonderful prospects," the pale face remarked. The Indian awakened from his dream and replied, "Yes, yes, and a strange, sad history." Within the next five minutes the fact was revealed that the Indian had lived for years as the foster child of an old acquaintance and close friend of the pale face missionary who now addressed him. The Indian was Dr. Nachita, and he wept great tears of joy. "The train is coming. I leave you now; help me to find my lost sisters," he begged the missionary, who replied, "I will search every corner of this locality; I know the Indians; my work has been among them; I will employ every means at my command and I will report success or failure." As the train thundered up to the station the two men exchanged names and addresses. Dr. Nachita clasped the hand of the stranger, boarded the train and was gone. The pale face, Rev. Silas Sheldon, began a long and patient search among the Indian tribes for the lost sisters. For a time the task appeared hopeless; then he wrote the doctor, after many weeks, "This I have learned upon reliable authority; your sisters were both adopted by Senora Cardoso, the wife of a wealthy Mexican miner of Sonora. My labor calls me into that locality. I shall investigate every clue. Many changes there have been since you were taken from your family upon that awful night. The people of this region keep no vital statistics, but I have hope; I shall make every possible effort. The Indian who furnished the clue also said he was told that Senora Cardoso adopted many children, and the family had moved about some." Months later Rev. Silas Sheldon wrote, "I have traced your sisters and find they both died years ago. The foster mother was deserted by her wealthy husband who married a beautiful young girl and left Sonora. The foster mother also disappeared, leaving no trace; but it seems she adopted among other children a boy; I am upon his trail; he will know the whereabouts of the little boy your oldest sister left." Dr. Nachita replied, "Find the boy; send him to me; don't let him slip through your fingers. I am willing to give up all I possess and start life all over, if only I can have my sister's child; I long to do for him what the pale face has done for me. This is the one link that binds me to the past; give me this boy and I will educate him and help him to be a good man; a worthy Indian; an honor to my race." Three months passed, during which time Dr. Nachita heard only once from Rev. Silas Sheldon, as follows, "I am tracing even slight clews; have many exciting and interesting experiences; have patience, doctor." Then one evening months afterward, into the doctor's office walked the Rev. Silas. "The boy! What of him? Tell me," cried the doctor with excitement, fear and hope all written upon his face and in his manner. "Yes, it is a long story full of thrills," the missionary continued. "It led me far into Mexico and to the door of many adobe homes. Once I was sure success had crowned my efforts. My Spanish interpreter came running headlong into the hotel where we stopped. 'I have found the child! I have found him,' he stammered. 'The mother gave him to a family living fifty miles away, and just recently they have moved into town. The foster father will bring the boy here and turn him over to you for twenty dollars.' 'Go tell him,' I said, 'that I will await him here and the money will be paid when he delivers the boy into my care.' Evening came and so did the Mexican with the child, a bright-eyed, healthy, intelligent youngster. Well, doctor, I was so overjoyed I could not maintain a semblance of dignity; I fairly danced about the room. 'I will send him to Dr. Nachita on the first train, early in the morning by the first train going north.' I sang this song and gave thanks all through the evening. I kept the little fellow close beside me; I feared some trick planned to extort more money; I held him in my arms for hours, and slept with him at my side. Morning came—after a wakeful night—and as I was preparing to go to the depot, again the Spaniard came running pell-mell, greatly excited and out of breath. He scarcely could speak. 'Wait! Wait!' he stammered; 'don't send the boy to Dr. Nachita; we are the victims of a ruse. The boy you are seeking died nearly a year ago. This is a Mexican child; he is one of a very large and very poor family. An Indian woman exposed the fraud to me. She learned what was being done and said, "Me no let them fool Indian doctor that way." ' "

Dr. Nachita leaned forward with his head resting upon his hands throughout the narrative, listening eagerly and longing for a ray of hope—a message from the past. When the Rev. Silas Sheldon finished his story, the Indian who had lost every relative on earth uttered no sound, but deep lines were on his face and great tears fell from his eyes, and he had found one more noble, loyal pale face friend. One more link had been forged in the brotherhood of man; and in God's garden bloomed another rare plant—Friendship.

CHAPTER XIII

A MIDNIGHT CALL

The doctor sat dreaming in his dusky den; always dreaming of the Indians out upon the plateaus and down in the dark valleys of the rock-ribbed West. The telephone bell rang: Tonto called, "Come quick, doctor, Chiquita is sick; you can help her; come to the old place; where we lived before we went among the Indians." "Yes! Yes! I am coming! Be quiet, Tonto; it is probably nerves; I say the illness, it may be only nerves; artists are high-strung folks, you understand." He hung up the receiver, caught up his coat and hat and put them on as he ran into the street.

There was no sign of street cars in either direction, so he jogged along on foot, and found Tonto waiting at the entrance of a tall, delapidated rooming house. They climbed the long stairs and groped along the dim corridor, Tonto leading the way to a small, poorly-lighted room on the third floor. There upon a dull brown couch lay the beautiful wife of Tonto. She was clad in a dainty robe of pale pink and her black hair tumbled about her fine head and shoulders in fluffy waves. When they entered Chiquita lay apparently asleep. "What seems to be the trouble?" the doctor asked. "Worry! worry! doctor. Chiquita knows her worth. She is a great actress, but the managers they know nothing of art. They do not appreciate Chiquita's gifts." At that moment Chiquita raised her head, extended a jeweled hand, and faintly smiled. Her low, rich tones thrilled the listener when she said, "Hubby dear was so kind to call you, and you were so kind to come. I suffer much at times. Just now I am comfortable." "My! my!" the doctor mused, "she might have been a queen, a princess, or anything that called for beauty and languid charms." "She must have rest and quiet; her nerves are exhausted; give up the stage for a little time and rest," he advised. Chiquita raised herself and sat up. "Yes," she said, "that is what we plan to do. We are going West and live with the Indians. I am tired of the white people. Tonto says his people will love me and make me their princess. I hate managers and actors. I still have money and we will go and live the real Indian life."

When they parted at the entrance, Dr. Nachita said, "Tonto, my boy, you were fortunate in having more than your share of good looks. Chiquita is a charming woman, but not over strong, and she has known the gilded side of life. You have a difficult position, Tonto. Do your best. Remember we are Indians, and prejudice has wrecked Chiquita's stage career. Perhaps it will be well to go among the Indians." Tonto hurried back to the dingy rear room, and Chiquita poured out a torrent of ill-humor upon the managers and stage folks.

"Think of it, Tonto, I played with the best actors, the very best! Who have they now playing my parts? Third-rate dummies! Tonto, I want the free, unrestrained life of the Indians. I long for the mountains. I shall smother in this stuffy place."

Tonto spoke slowly: "Well, Chiquita, you can be a queen out there. Many Indians are fine. Look at Dr. Nachita. I am proud of him. And Starlight is a noble woman. There are few like Starlight. She sings like the birds."

"O, hubby, dear, let us go. Let us go! I shall go mad in this room. Why did I leave my own dear land? I do not know. My family are proud and rich. The people there love art, real art, such as mine. The mountains are always near-by, and the skies are never clouded. Always a deep, deep blue, and I was happy and carefree."

Tonto knelt beside the couch, kissed her fervently and whispered, "Chiquita, dear girl, are you tired of me?"

"O, no, no, Tonto," she sobbed, "only this little room seems like my grave. Pack the few traps and let us go from here by daylight."

Her wish was law. But as Tonto moved about the room, his face was sad and he thought, "How can I keep pace with this marvelous creature? But I will try," he murmured very softly, "Chiquita is the wild flower, the rose, the lightning, and the avalanche; she is all nature combined." In the morning they departed long before daybreak; left the dirty, noisy city for the wild and glorious West, with glad hearts.

CHAPTER XIV

Life in the Open

For months Chiquita and Tonto had journeyed westward across the plains. Mounted upon small brown ponies they rode from camp to camp, lingering a week here, and a month there, until the high-strung Spanish beauty was weary of it all. The heat and dust, and the glaring sunlight had told upon her spirits. Even the gorgeous sunsets that caused her to cry out in amazement when first she beheld them, had now grown commonplace, and she was sad and very weary when at dusk one evening they rode into a small Indian village, in a picturesque spot upon the bank of a rapid river. "O, hubby dear," Chiquita cried, "this is the place for us to take root. The scenery is wild and grand. The Indians are fine, handsome fellows. The air is delicious and I am starved."

And so they bought a tiny ranch adjoining the camp and pitched their tepee. "I will weave baskets and embroider moccasins, hubby dear," she tossed her beautiful head and continued. "I will make the people love me, Tonto. I will sing the Indian songs, and I will learn their dances. I will be an Indian, Tonto," but Ah-ee! Ah-ee! prejudice and jealousy beset them even here among the Indians, at the foot of the great dark mountains, where to the casual observer all was simple and natural. Chiquita was fascinated by the dances; the crude, fantastic symbolism appealed to her imitative genius, and she threw herself into the Indian ceremonials with vivacity, and brought down upon her head the suspicion and contempt of every woman in the camp. They shot dark, angry glances toward Chiquita, they drew away and clung close to their men. Chiquita and Tonto kept open house and assisted every poor Indian who came to their tepee. But she was a white woman; what did they know or care about her great talent? Her beauty was dangerous; she was of another order of being.

Tonto said to the agent, "Why are Indians not subject to state laws? No man is a citizen unless subject to the laws of the state in which he lives. The Indian should be freed from supervision and compelled to obey the laws, or feel the lash of the laws until he knows that consideration for the rights of others is the basis of peace."

Chiquita said to the agent, "You have no right to build a jail on the reservation, and with the assistance of these Indian lackeys imprison the Indians at your own will. It is not fair and just. They are human beings. This whole land once belonged to them. They should be citizens."

"You talk too much," replied the Indian agent. "You are not wanted here. You and your old man better clear out. If you don't, I will see that you find it mighty uncomfortable. I am managing the Indians on this reservation and I have the entire government back of me."

"We will go," Chiquita cried. So they mounted their ponies at daybreak and rode away with scarce a farewell word or backward glance.

CHAPTER XV

The Pow-Wow

The house was brilliantly lighted, for Dr. Nachita that night entertained his friends—Indian and pale face. There met a motley crowd—artist, musician, writer, student and philosopher, and the face of the host glowed with pride and pleasure.

"To entertain people who know something is more satisfaction than to collect a bill from a professional dead-beat," he said, with that spontaneous, explosive mirth peculiar to the healthy boy. At these functions Dirk Danhoff was the doctor's right-hand man, for Dirk was a born comedian, and had been raised with the Indians; he had been admitted to the secret lodges and knew their rituals and ceremonial dances and songs. Dirk mimicked all that impressed itself upon the vision or hearing, and the doctor said he knew more about Indians than any white man living. Dr. Nachita brought in the tom-tom and instantly the place was changed into an Indian lodge. The call sounded upon the drum, and led by Dirk, the Indians swung into a dance that represented the graceful, alert, shy movements of the wild deer in the forest. The drum marked the rhythm of the dance, while the singing imparted a sense of gaiety and agility. At the close of this dance Dirk darted from the room and came back with one of the doctor's Navajo blankets and a green and red silk scarf. The latter he bound about his head and pulled a great shock of red hair down over his forehead, wrapped himself in the gay blanket, and then began the Medicine Dance. Other dances followed, and the pow-wow was in full swing. Chief Thundertalk was present and gave terse explanations of the meaning of each dance, which he said usually represented the movements of some animal or bird, and given by the primitive

Indians amid natural surroundings, in native costume, were deeply impressive.

After the Indian songs, dancing and drum accompaniments, a beautiful half-breed woman recited her own Indian poems, with a degree of grace and feeling that brought a flood of tears. Then followed what Chief Thundertalk called "the civilized music," and in his voice one detected the old scorn and derision. "The civilized music" turned out to be Cadman Indian songs, artistically sung by a pale face woman. But, ye gods, listen! Madam Yetta Leyden, a concert pianist, was there—one of the most temperamental of pianists. All this Indian color and dancing, intoning and drumming, swaying and tipping and bending, had aroused her musical soul. After giving an elaborate description of the incidents that preceded the composition, and led the composer to immortalize the scene in music, she sat at the piano and played Liszt's Rhapsody Number Six, with a fire and force that carried the doctor far away into the clouds, caused him to dream strange dreams, and awakened new impulses. Gypsies seemed flying through the air. Strange voices called to him. He was no longer the Indian—Pale Face philosopher. He loved fair and talented women; no longer the well-poised stoic. He looked about him, upon the faces of the little company and meditated in eloquent silence. "Color be hanged! the white women are simply wonderful! I love them all—understand—well, nearly all. Isn't she fine? Isn't she fine? Isn't she fine? My! My! Who cares about being a mere Indian? The fellow who clings to the old life will never arrive, understand."

The doctor did not really say these things aloud, but it was all written on his face. The Indian Princess—did she ever exist? Well, the beautiful dark lady in beads, and head-band, and inky black braids, and gay striped over-dress, and sad, demure Indian ways, arose and mentioned going. "O, no! No! No! No!" protested the doctor. "Come! Come! This way—everybody assemble in the den. Come! Come!"

In the doctor's Indian lodge they assembled about the big table, and there beneath the many eloquent reminders of a departed civilization, the little company sat down and partook of a dainty repast from choice hand-painted china and cut-glass. Some there were who felt the tragedy of the passing of that primitive life, some who looked into the sad faces upon the walls and understood; whose eyes rested upon an Indian cradle and whose memory called up from the dim past the life that once encompassed that bit of willow wand and grass, and heard the voices wafted upon the wind down through the years. While all through the hour Chief Thundertalk regaled the guests with Indian interpretations of the White Man's philosophy. Ordinarily calm and silent, the half-breed poetess now gives vent to bursts of mirth that justify her self-imposed sobriquet—the Wild Woman.

From a dark corner Dr. Nachita dragged a pet cat; a great handsome fellow—his special object of lavish affection. He coddled and held the cat while the guests ate—perhaps because thirteen sat at the table, and this extra number broke the spell.

The company returning to the drawing room marveled at the surroundings of the full-blooded Indian, which disproved the stories they recalled of the Red-man and his lair. Madam Yetta had departed and Dirk Danhoff staged a clever impersonation; he assumed a feminine and foreign manner and announced:

"I always preface my performances with an explanation; the composition I will now render represents Gods and Devils; incidentally the Gods and Devils get somewhat mixed."

He took his place at the piano and played variations of the Rigoletto Quartette, with madam's gestures and original ones by Dirk. The Wild Woman was roaring, when he sprang from the piano, ran to Dr. Nachita and closed the performance with an exact reproduction of madam's words and accent, "Ven I play vor you again, you mus' furnish me better piano, one big concert grand; some keys no work, and it is so aggravate." The imitation was perfect. The Wild Woman gave signs of convulsions, and the guests departed in a mild spring shower. As the last one passed out Dr. Nachita said, "In Sunday School they told me about the angels; to-night I have been among them. Don't forget to come back."

If during the progress of the reception a patient chanced to call, a singular scene occurred. The patient was halted at the entrance, and Dr. Nachita ran with a big cumbersome screen, which he adjusted to shield the caller from the eyes of the guests. The screen had seen long service and might have told interesting tales of the coming and going of many people of various colors and shades. Its wine-colored baize was soiled and faded, and the manner in which the doctor hustled it around proved long and close familiarity. At one time it was adjusted to form a corridor leading to the library. It might fence off the reception room. Again it was dragged the length of a long hall and partitioned off the telephone, if some one sat at the 'phone. There was no end to the uses the doctor had for this aged screen. Occasionally it toppled partly over, when too hastily adjusted, but the doctor had shot down the hall in the lead, and horror of horrors, the guests actually saw the patient—maybe a dark-skinned foreigner or a pale mulatto. Patients were distributed the length of the house—in the library—the den—sleeping chambers—and kitchen—possibly depending upon their social standing. No East Indian juggler could surpass the doctor's manipulation of the big screen. Not only mystery, but a touch of tragedy, clung to this article of furniture, in its journeyings up and down and across the hall, for Dr. Nachita, big of heart and sensitive beyond belief, was protecting his patient from race prejudice—from color prejudice—and yet prejudice is in reality not against color, but against mental characteristics—customs—environments. When these are made to harmonize, color prejudice disappears. Color is confounded with race differences in the minds of most people. Dr. Nachita was the soul of kindness, and to his mind the screen jugglery afforded a solution to the problem. But through haste and long habit he had grown careless and left gaps and openings, at times, through which the party in the reception room saw plainly the party passing behind the screen, and the affair dwindled into a farce—a useless expenditure of time and energy—except that the patient placed a world of confidence in the wisdom and caution of the big Indian doctor, who shielded his patients from public prejudice, which he branded, "a form of tyranny equalling that of the kings and barons of any age or country."

Not only was the doctor's home a mecca for all Indians stranded or not stranded; but many an impostor and fake Indian actor and actress found Dr. Nachita an easy prey. He could not refuse a call for help—and so the money flowed in and out from his pocket, as the procession passed through his bachelor quarters. Of course, they all loved him and told him so, and "crocodile tears" flowed freely when the caller was a stranded beauty who possessed great talent and hard luck.

Big-hearted Dr. Nachita! All are richer for having known him; the Indian who gathers to himself even sick, homeless cats.

CHAPTER XVI

THE INDIAN'S GOD

At sunset they rode due south, along a narrow valley with the mountains close upon their right. "Look, Tonto, there is an opening between the mountains down yonder. See how the light shines through; it looks like a great shaft of light coming through an open casement into a dark room." Chiquita's voice had the old child-like buoyant ring. They rode on for a short distance and suddenly came out into the bright crimson sunlight. They had reached the opening in the mountains, and there, as through a window, they saw the setting sun. Dismounting, they climbed a ledge of rock that shelved out into the gateway between two valleys. Above a great sea of misty shadows, and dimly outlined mountain peaks, the crimson sun was dipping downward. "Look! Look! Tonto," she pointed toward a little shining stream that coiled among the dull greens and grays and was lost in the shadows. "Just like a silver ribbon," murmured Chiquita.

Beyond the valley the dim outlines of jagged mountains were penciled through the dusky vapor, and through the air the rays of gold and crimson and violet quivered and shifted. Far out upon the rocky ledge—one foot upon its very brim—Tonto stood erect, with bared head. Chiquita raised both hands and cried, "Superb! Enchanting! Wonderful! Such color! Just like dear sunny Spain where the mountains and valleys and the sunsets are always glorious! Why did I come away?" A tremor passed through her body and she wept, all unheeded by Tonto, who was lost in wonder and surprise. They lingered spellbound, while the crimson and gold sank into purple and gray. Then out from the stillness came the sound of a little silver bell. "Ding—dong—ding— dong" the clear tones drifted through the waves of light and echoed down the narrow valley. Back and forth from peak to peak the sounds were tossed—"Ding—dong—ding—dong," in measured rhythmic cadence.

The sun disappeared and darkness crept over the valleys. As Tonto assisted Chiquita from the ledge, he whispered, "That was the Indian's God performing a miracle. Now we must hurry on—we lingered too long. The bell, I think, is on up that trail—we will follow." In a moment they had remounted and were climbing up a sloping path. The bell had ceased ringing when they rode out upon a small plateau and saw lights. The bell had led them to a little mission that clung to the rocks. Off toward the south a camp-fire flared up against the dark sky, and here and there great stars were stationed like night sentinels. The old padre had gone on a mission to the village not far away, and the French cook was alone. She welcomed the night wanderers and spread a royal feast of vegetables, and wild game, and honey. They had not tasted food since early morning, for they had journeyed all day through an uninhabited country, hence the little mission was a real haven for them. "Do not be afraid when the night owls hoot and the wildcats cry," the good cook said, "they are always with us up here. After awhile you listen for them, and would be a bit lonesome without them." Tonto laughed. "I was raised with wild animals," he replied.

On the following morning they were down in the valley upon the trail, when the old cook rung the matin bell at six o'clock. Chiquita had said, "We must hurry, Tonto. A strange illness is upon me." The sun was high up toward the zenith and it was near noon when they reached an Indian village where Tonto had friends. A tall chief welcomed them to his lodge close by a little river that came tumbling down from the mountains. "O, hubby dear, this is charming," Chiquita murmured.

And here it was that the little Wawa first opened his dark, sad eyes upon the big world. "We will call him

'Wawa,'" Chiquita said, "for when he came I thought of Dr. Nachita. That is the doctor's Indian name. By and by we will give him another name by which the world will know him." The Indians were very kind and shared with Tonto all they possessed. There was no agent nearby, and the women of the lodge were old, and quite deaf. After a few days all the able-bodied men took the trail in search of wild game. Tonto joined the hunt, from which they returned heavily laden. A great fire was kindled and the flesh of bear and deer roasted upon sticks in the old-fashioned way. Chiquita was quite happy. Tonto's share of the pelts would bring quite a little sum. Her money was exhausted and she had tired of Indian life. Those primitive people could never understand moody, impetuous, big-hearted, artistic Chiquita. She had placed herself beyond the pale of both Indian and white race. She no more comprehended her position than did the silent, patient Indian women comprehend Chiquita's dramatic gifts.

Tonto sold the furs to a trader and they were about to leave when word came that his only relatives living two hundred miles away were in deep distress. Leepool, his cousin, was very ill. Two hundred miles was a small matter to an Indian who possessed a good pony. So Tonto left Chiquita and the little Wawa with his friends and rode back toward the north. He covered forty miles of Indian trail and lodged for the night with a friend. The family slept outside in tepees. Tonto was given the "spare bed" in a log hut—their winter quarters which they would move into when the real cold nights came. The "spare bed" consisted of a rickety wooden bedstead, without furnishings save a pair of rusty springs. Tonto spread out his horse blankets upon the springs and used his bag of horse feed for a pillow. Nearby, in a bunk against the wall, an Indian in the last stage of tuberculosis tossed about upon a bearskin, but Tonto slept through sheer exhaustion. Toward morning, however, he was aroused by strange, uncanny sounds that seemed to come from overhead, and underneath, and all directions at the same instant. The place was very dark. He raised himself upon one elbow and listened. Then he lay down and laughed outright—"Rats!" An army of them were scampering along the logs and sliding down the corners of the room. Tonto dismissed them from his thoughts and fell asleep; soon he was awakened from a dream where he was sliding down a steep bank into a rapid river. As he wakened he felt the bag of horse feed moving from beneath his head. He sprang up and planted both feet in a mass of oats upon the floor. The rats had gnawed into the bag and were carrying away his horse feed. He gathered up what was left into a blanket, took it outside where the pony was tied to a tree, placed it within reach of the horse and threw himself down upon the bare ground, drew the blanket over him and passed the early morning hours in peaceful slumber.

After breakfast his friends induced him to leave the pony, walk two miles to the railway station and go by train to within eleven miles of his destination, which advice he followed. It was after dark when he left the train and started over the rough wagon-road toward the little ranch of Wild Cherry, his mother's sister, and Leepool, her son. It was a lonely bleak trail, most of the way along a wide drainage ditch, but Tonto pulled his hat low down over his face, shoved his hands into his pockets and pressed onward. The messenger had said, "Leepool will die—the Medicine Man he say so." Tonto must reach them. Wild Cherry and the boy had been very kind to him when he was left motherless. He was thinking of these things when out from the black, still heavens descended one of those swift storms that strike terror through weak hearts in the north. A blinding flash of lightning would send a blaze of light over the landscape, and up from the ground straight before Tonto would spring black, horrid-looking creatures, then down they fell with the darkness. The deafening peals of thunder shook the very ground, then with the next flash of light up jumped the black creatures before him, only to sink back into the darkness. They were the charred and jagged stumps left after the clearing of the land. Tonto bent forward and staggered on, keeping the road as best he could. The rain fell in a little thin sheet from the brim of his hat and his soaked clothing weighed him down and impeded his progress. By and by the storm swept on past him and Tonto drove his body forward through mud and water as though determined to keep up with the storm. Then the sky cleared and all the stars came trooping out, and he saw a dim light shining through a little window. It was the log cabin of Wild Cherry and Tonto had arrived while Leepool yet lived. The door was unfastened. He knocked loud, no one answered, and Tonto lifted the iron latch and stepped inside. Wild Cherry, with great effort, lifted herself from a pile of skins. "O, Tonto! Tonto! Good boy! Where did you come from?" she wailed. "We got on until I catched an awful cold. Now I no go for milk and Leepool he more sick, poor boy!" Tonto threw off his outer garments still dripping from the shower, in one corner of the room lay Leepool upon a wooden bedstead. He was very pale and weak, but when Tonto grasped his thin hand and held it between his two warm palms, he smiled and said, "The Great Spirit must have sent you, Tonto. I am so glad."

Tonto bustled about and made a pot of tea and toast and poached three eggs. After they had all partaken of the frugal meal, he sat down beside Leepool and drew from his pocket a physician's thermometer. He took the sick man's temperature and his pulse with the aid of his watch. Tonto knew that hope was all powerful in restoring the sick. He assumed an air of authority and professional knowledge and said, "Leepool, the white man's Medicine Man tells by these instruments if the sick are to live or die; now these tell me that you will live; so now, old boy, you just pull yourself together and live. I am here to care for you; leave all to me." At one A. M. Tonto climbed up the ladder-like stairs to the one low-ceilinged room above the living-room. He hung his wet clothing about the stove pipe and lay down for a few hours' rest. On the following morning, by seven o'clock, he was on his way to a neighbor's for milk, a journey on foot of six miles, but what was this to Tonto when he knew the milk was the very best nourishment for Leepool in his weakened condition? That day he cut a huge pile of wood, cleaned up a bit, and cooked food for Wild Cherry and himself. Soon after daylight on the following morning he started for the little station eleven miles away in quest of groceries and a pane of window glass which was greatly needed to keep out the cold blasts which came from the north in the morning hours. The window had been broken by the wind during a heavy thunderstorm months before. He made the entire trip on foot over horribly rough roads and paths and carried back a big sack upon his back. What he saw in the eyes of those two lonely, sick Indians more than repaid Tonto for his weary tramp. The window was mended, the larder replenished, and Leepool dragged himself up in the bed and leaned against a pile of blankets and murmured softly, "This is the Christ spirit we hear about; Tonto is a great man; I must live and watch him." Wild Cherry nodded and smiled, and presently she slowly arose and sat by the blazing fire. "I am most well. Tonto good medicine man," she said.

One incident laid heavy upon Tonto's heart, but this he kept strictly to himself. On the train he had been robbed of fifty dollars, no doubt by the man who sat beside him while he slept. He had carried with him nearly all the money obtained from the trader, for if Leepool died he must bear the expense of the funeral. Leepool was on the road to recovery, but Tonto's funds were reduced so that it would be impossible for Chiquita to return to the great city. They must go to some town not so far distant.

Tonto buoyed up his own spirits with constant efforts to ameliorate the condition of Wild Cherry and Leepool. Four days had passed. The sad-faced Indian woman was moving about the cabin and trying to again take up her routine of cares, when into the little home stalked an officer with a warrant charging Wild Cherry with stealing clothing from the dead. Tonto was greatly shocked and knew not what to say. He had planned to leave them on the following morning, but how could he desert his only living relatives at such a moment? He had a smattering of law, along with his other schooling, and this appealed to him as an opportunity to test his ability. He carefully drew from Wild Cherry all the facts and patiently analyzed the details until he was firmly convinced that she was innocent of wrong-doing.

Wild Cherry and her son were the only Indians living in that township. They were surrounded by an ignorant class of whites. A neighbor had sent for her to come and care for his sick wife, while he toiled at wood cutting three miles to the north. Leepool also worked with the man. Wild Cherry had gone to the neighbor's cabin and remained with the sick woman for nine days and nights, and at the end of this long vigil the patient had died. During the last three days, Meg Meehen, who lived two miles away, had come to assist Wild Cherry, for the woman was growing worse. The doctor said there was no hope and the husband must work. While the two women were "laying out the body," Meg had said, "I wonder if he would sell me her clothes." "Don't talk so," Wild Cherry replied, "the poor woman is not yet cold, and to want her clothes is a sin."

When the end came Wild Cherry had hurried to the nearest neighbors for someone to go and bring the dead woman's husband. Meg was alone in the cabin at that time. Tonto walked the distance to and from this neighbor's cabin, timing himself by his watch and found that it took him three quarters of an hour to cover the ground, hence Meg's claim that "she had never been in the cabin a minute alone," was proven false. Then Tonto began an inquiry as to Meg's reputation and found that she was considered a thief at the general trading store eleven miles away, where he bought the groceries. The owner told him that he was compelled to watch his goods always when Meg Meehen came in, for he had caught her several times trying to make 'way with articles. Tonto also found that Meg's husband had been arrested once for theft.

With all the evidence carefully written out, Tonto took with him two neighbor men and began a careful search behind stumps and logs near the Meehen cabin and was rewarded by finding a part of the missing clothing secreted in a hollow log. The case was called and Tonto appeared as Wild Cherry's defender. The Indian could not employ an attorney without permission from the Indian department, and this would require a delay of many days. The trial was held down at the station, just three days from the date of indictment.

Tonto laid his evidence clearly and concisely before the judge and questioned Wild Cherry as to all the little details she had already explained to him. He exhibited the clothing they had found in the woods near the Meehen home. Wild Cherry was a large, heavy-set woman and would be unable to wear a single garment that had belonged to the dead woman. He proved by the neighbor that Wild Cherry had been gone from the cabin for well on toward an hour, while Meg was alone with the corpse. By his questioning of Meg and her husband he drew suspicion down upon their heads as to their general character and their reputation as thieves. The outcome was that Wild Cherry was acquitted, and later Meg and her husband were indicted for grand larceny by a merchant in the next township.

Tonto said good-by to Leepool and Wild Cherry and started on his long journey back to Chiquita. He felt rather guilty for having left his wife and baby among strange Indians for so long. In due time he reached the lodge where he had left his pony. Once mounted and out upon the trail, the events of the preceding days came out clearly before his mind and Tonto said aloud:

"Money we must have, at least enough to exist on, but there are things which money cannot buy. That poor Indian woman no doubt would have lost her little homestead had she been left to the mercy of her white neighbors. And Leepool surely would have died without proper nourishment and a new grasp upon hope."

The value and power of justice stood out in Tonto's mind as never before, and the helplessness of the uneducated, isolated Indian had never occurred to him as at this moment.

It was a long, dreary journey, but at last it came to an end just at nightfall, when Tonto rode up to the lodge of his Indian friends and found Chiquita suffering one of her old spells. Never before since childhood had Tonto visited the Indian homes in winter. When he left for the north the family were living outside on the river bank in tepees. During his absence the weather had turned cold and twelve people, including Chiquita and the baby, were huddled in one large room. The aged grandmother of the family sat crouched over the fire, picking her sore eyes. The oldest son was coughing incessantly with tuberculosis, scattering the dangerous germs about the ill-kept and overheated room. Tonto felt sure that the temperature of the room was over one hundred, and he soon made an excuse to go outside and look after his horse. In reality, he felt that he must go outside in search of fresh air. He was not long in coming to a decision. If Chiquita was able, they would leave in the morning.

When Chiquita awakened from her long, heavy sleep, she was in bad humor. Tonto had stayed away a long time, she pouted. The little Wawa was pale and ill. "Life in this hovel is an inferno. I was happy outside with the birds and trees, but now the weather is cold and we must stay inside. They are filthy. The children have vermin. That man huddled in the corner and the six-year-old boy have consumption. The agent says the old women have trachoma. What the dickens that is, I don't know, but I am going away from here, Tonto. I am sick of grit in my food. The agency doctor says we will lose Wawa if we stay here. More than half the Indian children die. Some women lose all their children, and yet the stupid creatures keep on propagating. What chance have the children?"

Tonto looked at the babe in Chiquita's arms, and then he began to pack into a sack what few articles they possessed. When they rode away Chiquita carried the child upon her back, strapped to an Indian cradle.

CHAPTER XVII

A Passing Cloud

The door-bell rang violently. Dr. Nachita dropped the tablet on which he was writing and hurried to admit his caller. A small boy who was very much out of breath, and frightened.

"Come, doctor," he said, "they got Starlight in jail."

"My, my," Dr. Nachita exclaimed, "what are you telling me, boy? Starlight in jail? What for? How?"

Without waiting for an answer he started with coat and hat in hand. The boy took him straight to the little home where Starlight had lived with the baby and the old nurse. Dr. Nachita rushed in, and standing before the woman exclaimed:

"What has happened? This boy tells me Starlight is in jail. Where is the baby?"

The old woman replied in a tense, high-keyed voice:

"I know nothing, only a tall woman came with an officer. She said Starlight had stole the baby—her brother's child. She took the young one away and the officer took Starlight. I have no place to go so I stay here."

"My! My! This is awful," cried Dr. Nachita, "Starlight, poor girl! I brought this all upon her. Whoever dreamed of such a calamity."

By this time he was down the steps and headed toward the nearest police station, where he learned that Starlight had been booked on a charge of kidnaping.

"My! My! Kidnaping! Whoever heard of such a thing? Starlight! Why, that girl wouldn't kidnap a flea. Where is she? I must see her at once."

A bailiff led him down a long corridor to the cell of Starlight.

"My! My! Think of such nonsense and injustice, all because she is an Indian girl." He stormed along the corridor to Starlight's cell, but when he looked upon the girl's haggard face, all his Indian bravery was aroused. No sound escaped the lips of Starlight, but pride and scorn flashed from her dark eyes.

"I will bring the best attorney that money can command and we will fight this to a finish," the doctor shouted, and fire shot from his big eyes. Then for the first time the bitter, humiliating thought occurred—The Reservation Indian cannot engage an attorney for self-defense without the consent of the Indian agent and the Department of the Interior. Starlight to exist in this filthy dark place until that is accomplished? No! Never! "I will call my white friends to her assistance. I will return and in the meantime, understand, Starlight, that I am not idle."

In an incredibly short space of time Dr. Nachita appeared before Judge Thoroughgood, accompanied by two influential citizens, and also the woman who had taken the babe from the dying mother's arms and later carried it to the doctor's home.

"Lock me up, judge, but let that innocent girl Starlight go," he cried, "it is all a mistake! The mother, when dying, begged me to find Starlight and give the child to her if she would accept the responsibility. The father had often said, 'Starlight is the noblest, best woman in all the world.' The mother felt that Starlight would be a safe person to trust with this responsibility, partly because she knew that once Starlight had loved the father of her child.

"Judge, this Indian girl has a great future before her, and this is a deep injustice. She entertains a peculiarly bitter sentiment toward the pale face for certain well-founded reasons, understand, and I thought to wipe out this bitterness by having Starlight become attached to the little helpless white babe. My plan was that the whole affair should result in general uplift, understand, but my! my! it failed to work out right. The child was brought to my home by this woman beside me. She is the woman who took the child from the arms of the mother before she died. I labored for some little time to convince Starlight, and when she accepted my viewpoint I immediately placed the infant in her arms, and here poor Starlight has landed in jail. This is awful! awful! judge. You see, I have lived with the white people for many years, judge, and I am of the opinion that nothing will wipe out the ill-feeling between the two races except close association. We must all have the same training, the same interests, the same education—then the Indian problem disappears. The whites must give up their prejudice against the Indian and treat him as a human being. Think of that abominable aunt—she never had seen the child—never had contributed one penny toward the support of the baby. In fact, I did not know that the child had a single relative; and think of her pouncing upon Starlight and having her jailed. And I, you understand, was the guilty party, if guilt there was. It came about, understand, through my desire to produce harmony. The whole miserable condition of the Indian to-day is the result of misunderstanding between the two races. It is a long, sad story, judge, and I would be as bitter as the average member of my race, understand, had I not lived with the pale face from childhood."

"Well, Dr. Nachita," the judge began with deliberation, "I understand there was an entire absence of premeditated wrong-doing in this case. Just a lack of foresight as to possible consequences. Of course, you people are not well informed as to state and federal laws. I understand the education of the Indian along this line has not been what it should be, but the majesty of the law must be upheld. The accusing party invoked the law without sufficient evidence to substantiate the indictment. I desire to be humane and just in view of the existing facts a priori. I shall dismiss the case—it being a *propos de rien.*"

"Well, judge," Dr. Nachita interposed, "does Starlight get out of jail?"

"Yes, that is the direct and express object of my contemplated procedure, Dr. Nachita."

"Well, I appreciate your attitude, judge, and I admit that I know very little about law, although I have lived the white man's life for about fifty years, but I do recognize justice and fairness when I meet it. And Starlight must not suffer for my blunders—if blunder there was, understand—I leave that for you to decide, judge."

Judge Thoroughgood questioned the witnesses who accompanied Dr. Nachita, and the interview brought about the release of Starlight on the following day. She went back to the little home and the old nurse and refused to discuss the incident even with Dr. Nachita.

CHAPTER XVIII

Breaking Camp

Unusual signs of life were visible about the Indian quarter of a western town. Rev. Tobias Waring who was superintendent of the Indian Mission, had brought to the village a concert company for an afternoon concert in the Mission House. There were four ladies in the company; one of them a niece of the Rev. Mr. Waring. The quartette had "come some distance out of their way to sing at the Indian Mission." When the hour arrived the Indians entered the building stepping very softly, and sat upon the wooden benches in silence. The men sat on the left and the women upon the right side of the room. A female concert company, appeared to the Indians a queer innovation. The elder ones growled, and one ventured to say, "Indian woman no sing for show; Indian woman no travel all 'lone." But the smiling faces of the four singers, and their beautiful voices soon disarmed even the old men and women, and their faces lost their sadness. Forgotten was their hatred for the pale face, while their souls were lifted up above the dreary reservation atmosphere, and they drew a trifle nearer the pale face. While they sang the eyes of the quartette roamed among the dusky faces, and there their leader, a tall blonde girl, found a familiar face. It was the face of Chiquita, the once famous actress, now changed almost beyond recognition. The blue eyes of the blonde met the black eyes of her old acquaintance. A faint smile passed over the features of the dark woman who sat in the rear row of seats dressed in deerskin skirt and moccasins and faded shawl. She whispered to a tall Indian man beside her, and they left the Mission House. At the close of the concert the blonde girl ran to the Rev. Tobias Waring and asked, "Who are the couple who left the hall while we sang?" "They are strangers here; the wife is a white woman; they wander among the tribes. I hear the woman was once a great actress." The blonde kept her own council, but stole away and roamed among the tepees. Out upon the border of the camp she found Chiquita. They were making ready to take the trail. Tonto gathered their belongings; Wawa rolled in the sand before the door of the tepee, while Chiquita lay inside on a blanket upon the ground, smoking a cigarette. The blonde girl had seen Chiquita upon the stage, in the great roles; seen her arrayed in gorgeous robes and decked with costly jewels. She had listened when Chiquita's deep, mellow-toned voice moved vast audiences to tears—and this woman? Could it be that she was the same Chiquita, whose small shapely feet she had seen covered with jeweled slippers or shod in dainty boots that cost fabulous prices? The moccasins upon this woman's feet were old and shapeless and filthy. "Come in!" Chiquita called to her visitor, in a low coarse voice, as she raised herself upon one elbow and rolled over. "Tell my fortune?" The blonde smiled and held out a silver dollar. Chiquita sat up and commanded, "Sit down." The blonde with awkward movements dropped down upon the ground. Chiquita held out one hand for the money, and began to prophesy: "You will marry for love, and poverty will camp upon your trail." She looked into the blonde's palm and went on: "Sickness will come and love will vanish, then you will go back to your music and find contentment, which is the most we may hope for; but we must love first; there is no escape; it is woman's fate until she is freed from self; I guess love is about all there is for woman anyway. Marry one with ideas, and ambition; otherwise you starve. Love dies out and then you will find life aimless and hopeless, but stick to your music as long as you have ambition; but Great Peter, what use telling you anything; you will obey your feelings, and love masters all. Later on you may reason a trifle, maybe not. A letter is on the way; a dark woman crosses your path;

that may prove to be a black dog. You will go on a long journey and meet a tall man." Chiquita was groping for words, groping for ideas when suddenly the blonde said: "Chiquita, come away from this life. You have changed. Come back before it is too late!" The woman who had voluntarily turned her back upon wealth and fame and civilization, who had tossed from her the marvelous gifts nature had lavishly bestowed upon her, replied mournfully: "It is already too late; the pale face rejected my Indian husband. When you have suffered much you are no longer blind and deaf; courage and hope are gone. The tragedies are not all upon the stage. My ambition—my pride and my health are gone; we have lingered here a long time; we buried my second baby out there beside that brush, where I can see the grave from the door of the tepee. The money is gone now and we must move on." She looked up at the face of the blonde, and threw the stub of her cigarette upon the ground. She went on, "I have written a play about a white woman who married an Indian for love and lived happy ever afterward. I have learned the ways of the Indians. We are going into the show business as Indians. I have written the big managers and they never reply, but Tonto and I can manage to exist." "Why not sing, Chiquita? When you studied with Signor Badi we looked forward to hearing you in grand opera." "Yes, Tonto and I sing Indian songs in the play; we at least can live. The Indians don't want us here. The women are jealous, but I have learned their ways and I can earn my living in vaudeville as a squaw." She threw back her head defiantly and coughed. Deep lines were carved about the once beautiful mouth; the whole face and figure had grown heavy, dull and sensual. Only when she smiled one recognized the once fascinating actress who had been courted by famous men. The blonde looked down upon Chiquita's clumsily shod feet, and up at her unkempt hair, and her own blue eyes filled with tears. She got up from the bare ground, opened her purse and emptied it into the lap of Chiquita. "Accept it in memory of the days when we sang in the great professor's studio and looked forward to grand opera," the blonde whispered. Just then Tonto led the ponies up in front of the tepee and called, "Come on, Chick; we must be moving if we reach the Lodge of Barefoot to-night." They had lingered to hear the quartette. Chiquita and the blonde went outside, and Tonto pulled down the tepee and loaded the truck upon the backs of the ponies. The three rode away from the village unobserved, and the blonde girl ran back to the Mission House where Rev. Tobias had called an Indian policeman, and said, "Go, search for her."

At sunset the four singers left the camp en route to the railroad station a mile distant. When they reached the hollow at the foot of the hill below the mission, they all looked back, and there upon the hilltop stood the Indians huddled together; their dark forms outlined against the brilliant sky, and their long shadows reaching down into the hollow, silent and sad they watched the departure of the pale face, thinking of the beautiful songs and the sweet faces that had brought one pleasant hour into their long, dreary day. "This camp is well on the road toward civilization," said the Rev. Tobias Waring, who accompanied the quartette back to the railroad. "Last week we entertained an Eastern editor; he rode into camp with a black bear dangling from his saddle. I brought out my camera and demanded a picture of Mr. Editor and bear. While I adjusted the machine, the editor's horse became restless, probably the bear's foot touched the animal's side. Suddenly he reared, then threw down his head, and into the air shot Mr. Editor and Bruno, high over the head of the pony, and landed in the tall grass. A solemn-faced young Indian who stood nearby, threw himself down upon the ground and roared with mirth. The editor was unharmed and later I took the picture, but no doubt the Indian would have laughed had the pale face lain dead. Scorn and contempt for the stupidity of the white man rang in his voice and shone from his black eyes. They are a strange, unfathomable people until you know them; but once you know them, you know that the whole Indian problem is a misunderstanding on the part of both races." "If only I was an artist," the second alto said, "I would paint them, they are just grand; such tall, graceful, picturesque fellows." The blonde girl was silent. Tears were in her eyes, and all the while she looked about as though in search of someone lost.

CHAPTER XIX

The Down Grade

The Cabos were established in their old quarters in the big city. In the same dingy back room on the third floor of a rooming house, Chiquita stormed the "Wick-i-ups" of the theater managers, blustered and berated their lack of artistic appreciation, all to no purpose. One manager gave her a trial engagement, but he found her imperiousness unbearable. She would drop her voice down into the lower regions and order the furniture changed for the setting, the draperies removed, etc. "Take that out and bring me a blue drape. I want dull, red rugs; take them away at once." Two hours of Chiquita's imperialism closed the scene. The manager dismissed her with an oath. The adulation of Tonto had inflated the ego of poor Chiquita. She had grown coarse and bitter through experience with poverty and wild, aimless life among the Indians. Tonto's attraction was based upon his picturesque appearance. He was of colossal build, quiet and graceful and sang soft Indian love songs. The time came when her love had burned out, and then she found the Indian cold and indifferent, dull she thought, and yet she clung to him, for she was destitute and ill, and must exist. Her spirit was broken. Hope and ambition had fled; she had no courage or strength with which to struggle back to her former position, and she did not even see the way whereby this might have been accomplished. At times she suffered great bodily pain, and in affright she sought relief from drugs, thoughtlessly prescribed, for livelihood, by physicians unacquainted with her morbid tendencies. They had no resource save the little Indian playlet Chiquita had written while on the reservation. The dirty little tepee presented a pitiful scene to one who knew Chiquita's past. Tonto danced; a little dog frisked about an artificial camp fire and Chiquita squatted upon the ground and beaded a moccasin or pretended to cook a chunk of meat in the fire, while Tonto sang a strange Indian love song. Chiquita represented the typical squaw in blanket, beads and moccasins. In the bright yellow spot light she mimicked the Indian women who had hated her. One day Tonto met upon the street his friend, the Indian attorney. "Come to the show," he said, "and see our play. Chiquita wrote it." That evening the attorney went to a small, dingy, foul-smelling vaudeville house in one of the city suburbs, and witnessed one of the last dramatic attempts upon the stage of the once famous actress. He did not approve of the commercialization of the Indian. To him it was sad and pathetic; he had seen Chiquita in her famous characterizations of the great roles, when she gave promise of being the greatest known actress. He was shocked by her changed appearance.

The life of the tepee Indians never before had appeared so far away from his life. To Tonto he said, "Cabo, you are wasting your time at this business; you need strong, vigorous mental and physical exercise. Chiquita has worse than wasted her time and talent. Look around you; the type of people who are being amused by this fake presentation of Indian life are not the type that you should seek to please. They crave the morbid—the queer and irregular. They are dazzled by the light and color. They care nothing about the progress of our race. They have more interest in the painted clown, than they have in all the thinkers that time could produce. Thinking tires them. Tonto, get away from all this. Do something toward the uplift of our own race." "But we must live and at present there seems no other way." "Come with us to the train and speak with Chiquita of this matter," Tonto continued. "Wait only a few moments until I pack the traps." It was a long "few moments" before they appeared, Tonto with the tepee and all the other paraphernalia hanging over his shoulders, and Chiquita carrying the dog under her long cape. Her manner was gruff and insolent. Her few words were spoken in low, harsh tones and mixed with Spanish. She walked with a slow, swaggering gait. The attorney took her arm. When they reached the elevated station, as they ascended the stairs, her step became clumsy and halting, and the attorney found himself dragging and lifting the woman. When they reached the platform she fell sprawling upon the floor. "Run, Tonto, and bring a physician," the attorney said; but Tonto grinned and whispered, "O, this is nothing; she took a little too much from the bottle before we started." The attorney was shocked and feared they would be arrested when they reached the railway station, but Chiquita could not stand alone, and Tonto begged his friend to assist him in getting her aboard the train, otherwise they would miss their next engagement. Chiquita fell asleep and gave them little trouble until they reached the depot. They missed the train, and had a dismal wait of two hours, attended with much anxiety, at times, fearing an officer would take the intoxicated Chiquita from their care. Two A. M. arrived, after what the attorney thought the longest and most sad and humiliating experience of his life. He helped drag Chiquita into the car and hurried away, comparing the scenes of the evening that had passed with the night when he sought an introduction to Chiquita, for Tonto. "This is a terrible tragedy," he whispered; "it involves the whole Indian problem. That gifted, beautiful girl lost her position and prestige through prejudice for the Indian. It is a cruel fate. All her achievements fell to the ground because she loved an Indian. Had Tonto been a successful business or professional man would this have happened? I think not." He clinched his fists as he walked, and muttered, "The Indian must wring success from life, no matter what his handicap. He must have the where-with to more than exist before he takes a wife. Life for our people has grown deeply complicated. We are compelled to reckon with this complexity. Poor girl, how fascinating, how beautiful she was that night when Tonto spoke with her for the first time. It cuts me to the heart; I regret having gone with him to the play; I hope it is not too late; I hope Chiquita will give up this accursed stuff. Poor child! The Chiquita I saw that night at the big theater—she was of the fearless, impetuous, temperamental type. Tonto was calm and powerful physically. She plunged into the caldron of passion and dissipation and comes out a wreck. The price was too great—poor, thoughtless Chiquita! To know the laws that govern this life means to choose the best. I hope escape is possible for her. Sad! Sad! Reason and moral restraint we must have; otherwise. what we call love too often blinds and sears and destroys. The child is with Starlight; that is well; Starlight represents the nobility of our race."

CHAPTER XX

The Vision

Dr. Nachita raised one arm high above his head, waved his hand in salutation to an invisible host, clinched his fist, and brought it down upon the big square table with a bang! "The time has come," he shouted, "I must go to my people. I have lingered too long. A voice is calling me."

The heavy door drapery was lifted; the face of a pale, fair woman appeared in the opening, and a gentle voice exclaimed: "There, now, you have been banging that table again, and the quills and beads are scattered in every direction."

"Never mind the quills and beads," the doctor replied, "there are lots more where they come from. Get yourself ready for a long journey, Blue Bird. We start to-morrow."

"Why, you don't intend to scalp me and commit suicide, do you?" The doctor shook with laughter; the pet cat stretched her great length out upon the Navajo blanket in the corner of the davenport. "That's pretty good," the doctor continued. "No, no, nothing quite so bad as that, but we are going, Blue Bird. Mind, lose no time, we go to-morrow. I must get out into the open. These great piles of books and all this trumpery just simply stifle me. I want a glimpse of that golden sunset land, and I must see my people. I must talk with them. I must help them with their burdens. It is all wrong for me to sit here, dormant, acquiescent, enjoying the comforts and advantages of the great prosperous city, letting the precious hours drift away into eternity when I should be aiding my people. The time is not coming. The time for action has arrived. My race must arise! I say, my race must come up from the valley of black shadows into the broad light of day;"

Again he waved his arms, clinched his fists, and banged the table. "There you go again," cried Blue Bird, "what grudge have you got against the table? It will be falling to pieces."

"Get ready! Get ready! The tang of the wild is in my brain."

The doctor was a full-blooded Indian; this was quite obvious from his dark skin, straight black hair, and type of features. That he was a thinker, and entertained a great vision, was obvious likewise in the lofty bearing and dreamy expression of his eyes.

With wonderment we peer about the room he has left. It is a den; a museum of Indian mementoes; the doctor's retreat where alone he dreams of the past and writes long expostulations upon the causes which have led up to the present condition of the Indian race. Light that is soft-toned and weird, radiates from beneath a dull colored lamp shade and mingles with the dull red of the leather mat that covers the top of a massive oak table in the center of the room. From beneath the leather mat a beautiful Navajo spread falls over the table and down close to the floor, where Indian rugs lay in wait for noisy feet. Brown shadows fill the room, and many sad, dark faces look down from the walls, where every inch of space is covered with Indian pictures. Suspended by hooks and cords from the ceiling, many curious objects are swinging overhead. A pair of gray and blue-beaded moccasins, made by the famous Chief Geronimo; wampun bags adorned with eagle feathers and scalp locks; baby cradles heavy with beads; others made of simple strips of willow; strange decorations lavishly adorned with tiny mirrors, and eagle feathers, all arranged in one long strip which was worn about the neck of noted chiefs; worn by riders in the bright sunlight they were visible miles away, as the mirrors flashed back their many reflections, in those vanished days of pomp and glory; peace pipes "from the great red pipestone quarry" point their long, dull stems down toward the light. Various articles of pottery stand upon the sideboards, shelves and cabinets; beautiful jugs, bowls, and pitchers made by the Pimas and Mojaves; baskets of finest weave and most singular design nestle here and there, while bows and arrows swing dangerously low overhead. High on the wall hangs a tom-tom bearing a war scene upon its pale leather head; nailed to a door is a bear-skin with the stern, strong face of Chief Red Cloud painted upon its rough surface. Over the center of the table hangs a beaded cradle from the lodge of the chief whose eyes look at you from the bear-skin. Here among the gray shadows, and the dull red and brown and gold tints, Doctor Nachita dreams and ponders night and day of his people—their condition now and their prospects for to-morrow. When all alone he may take from its peg the tom-tom, place it upon a low stool before him, tap lightly upon its painted war scene and listen, while from the shadows of the past, merry dancers and grim stately warriors troop by. He sees great, dark, flashing eyes; tall willowy forms; feather-bedecked warriors mounted upon swift horses with gay trappings, rush past. He sees the camp-fire upon the mesa at night. He sees a low willow hut, and a mother with a babe at her breast. He hears voices chanting in low, monotonous cadences. Hunters ride past driving before them a herd of deer. On into a dark ravine they dash and are lost in the shadows.

Once more Dr. Nachita taps softly, gently, upon the mellow-toned drum; and then his eyes fill with tears. "All gone! All gone!" he murmurs. "It is a sad, sad story. My people! My people!" The drum gives out a deep-toned, soft, and slow boom! boom! The eyelids close and the drum stick falls down upon the Indian mat. A big black and white rabbit comes across the room and nibbles at his feet. He springs up, thrusts aside the tom-tom, strikes the table with his clenched fist, and roars, "Color be hanged! The Indians are obsessed by fear. If the Indian only would wake up and think for himself, and act for himself; work and learn; but some way he has been crushed and his spirit broken by years of fear and want. Wake up! Wake up! We are men like other men."

Blue Bird would lift the brown blanket that curtained the doorway, look in and call to him, "There you go again; you make my head ache, hollering about the Indians. Why not do something? And quit pounding the table."

Then Dr. Nachita would look up at the stern visage of Sitting Bull for a short time and go in silence to the little library where the books were piled tier upon tier close up to the ceiling. By and by he would write upon a big tablet with hurried movements, "I see the whole terrible tragedy passing before me. O God! I would forget. I cover my eyes. I try to shut out the dark picture, but it is always there before me. It haunts my dreams. The soul of my mother calls to me from the other world—'Child,' it says, 'lift up your voice; lift up your voice for your own; for your people.' I cannot forget until the morning dawns."

CHAPTER XXI

Her Tryst With Death

The rain fell in torrents upon the leaky roof of a hovel far out in the city's suburbs. From the one room a dim light streamed out into the darkness. The wind rattled the loose boards, sighed, and whistled by turns. Within this make-shift dwelling the gloom was appalling, for the Angel Death had entered and taken away the weary spirit of Chiquita. The place was wretchedly furnished; filthy and cold. Tonto knelt beside the couch where lay the body of the once beautiful and fortune favored Spanish actress. His arms were folded about the little Wawa, and between broken sobs he whispered, "Fate was cruel! Fate was cruel!" He laid his hand very gently upon the boy's dark head and looked into the eyes that were marvelously like those of Chiquita, when Tonto first beheld her. Wawa cried, "Mamma! Mamma!" At that moment the door latch was lifted and into the room stepped Starlight. She dropped her rain coat upon the bare floor and waited for Tonto to speak. In that moment of silence, the whole tragedy of the life that had passed, loomed up before her. She could scarce believe that Chiquita had closed her eyes for the last time in this hovel. The air was stifling. The shadows and gloom sent a chill through stout-hearted Starlight. Tonto arose, with tears falling from his eyelids. He tried to speak but his lips were dumb. "I am here to tell you, Tonto, I would gladly have nursed her had I known." Starlight's voice was very low and the sympathy of a great heart vibrated through each word. "Why did you not call me?" she questioned. After a long period of silence he replied: "Starlight, until last night I did not know that Chiquita was more ill than common; but the doctor came and said, 'The end is very near.' I was bewildered; I just sat and watched her breathing until it ceased. I thought, of course, this last spell was like the others—just morphine and whiskey. She suffered in mind and body; that is why she took the drug. Poor Chiquita, she gave up all the world for me; the sacrifice was too great; prejudice followed her like an evil spirit from the hour she smiled upon me. I am guilty, Starlight; I did not understand how much it would cost; love is selfish! Love is selfish, Starlight. I tried, but it has been hard to exist; I never dreamed that Chiquita would be ostracized because of my color. Starlight, I hate the pale face; poverty has clung to us and dogged our steps and now I must ask for aid at the very last hour; and Chiquita had fortunes at her command before she loved me." "You will ask no favors of white man or Indian," Starlight replied. "It is my privilege to assist you, but Tonto, do not breathe the word hate. Once bitterness and hate sank deep into my soul and caused me great suffering. Through the night hours my heart cried for revenge, and my lips cried, 'How can I, Starlight, a frail Indian girl, inflict cruel, sharp pain upon the object of my hatred?' I held these terrible thoughts, Tonto, until they nearly crushed out my life. At last I found a better, more profitable way; when I could no longer breathe the atmosphere of hate and revenge; when I found I must forget my wrongs or perish, ill in mind and body, I turned into a new sunlit trail. The light came suddenly. It broke in upon my soul one dreary day, when the clouds drifted from before the sun, and my room was flooded with bright light. I ran into the garden among the flowers and birds; I lifted my eyes to the blue of heaven and my heart sang, 'How blind! How deaf! There is nothing in this beautiful world worth having that is not mine! I have life—and strength—and time—time in which to change all that is wrong in myself and my environment.' The beauty of the world is mine—and Tonto, the world is beautiful when the eyes are not blinded by some destructive element like hate. To be emancipated from bitter thoughts; to vibrate in harmony with all life—this, Tontó, is the new birth. The fire I passed through consumed some element within me that was holding me down to earth; that stifled all that was best within me. It was a selfish animal—love—that I once thought necessary to my existence, but the love I now hold necessary to my life is never destructive. It is the higher love; the universal love that forgets, and hopes, and waits, and labors for the general welfare of the race." "O, I have nothing to live for," Tonto moaned. "You cannot die; there is no real death; Tonto, all is change, ceaseless change—nothing is lost when once created. The child—is he not worth living for? The Indian race, are they not worth struggling for? And, Tonto, you have much to live and labor for; a mighty responsibility rests upon each one of our race, and those who fortunately have received new light—some education, some mental development, must lead the way, must hold up the torch to light the footsteps of those less fortunate ones who grope in darkness." "Yes, Starlight, that is all good, but the pale face rejected Chiquita; my own people spurned her, and it cut her to the heart; it is so sad, so sad; they repudiated Chiquita; remorse gnaws at my heart. It was my fault. Why did I accept so great a sacrifice? She was adventurous, impetuous, thoughtless, and the ills all recoiled upon her." "But, Tonto, it is past; not one step backward may we take except in thought; we must move onward with the universe. There is great work to be accomplished; let us save from the past only its lessons. Chiquita is at rest—poor, tired heart. Purge your soul from the passion that helped to destroy the Chiquita you adored, and go forward into the future, a power for the emancipation of our race. Tonto, you studied law once; take that for your profession; master it. The Indians need strong defenders. They need powerful examples of success to inspire them to personal effort." She stepped to the bedside, lifted the tattered spread that covered the form of Chiquita, and laid upon the dead woman's breast a pure white fragrant lily. Then she turned her beautiful face toward the dim light and Tonto saw a glory shining from the eyes of Starlight—it was love and peace and hope, and by some mysterious influence, his soul was lifted up and strengthened, and hate and bitterness dwindled into nothingness. He saw the beauty and power of mental poise. Starlight was calm, and love radiated from her being even in the presence of death, and want and agony. Starlight went quietly about those tasks which the occasion brought to her hand. Tonto took the child and crept into the darkest corner where for a long time he sat in meditation. He recalled the time when their women made the night hideous with their lamentations for the dead; he had seen both men and women slash their bodies with knives, and cut off the hair and even the fingers, in token of grief. Was it not best after all to submit to the inevitable? Was it not the better way to keep command of the body? Here was Starlight, gentle, kind-hearted, noble Starlight, an Indian girl, going about calm and dignified in the presence of death. How crushed and helpless and bitter he felt at the moment of her coming. Now he was beginning to see the light. Poor, unhappy Chiquita had suffered much. After all, was it not best that she should have rest? Why, long ago she had attempted to end it all, and failed; but why must it all be so? He became confused in his reasoning and tried to stop thinking, but try as hard as he could to shake it off, remorse fastened its fangs into his flesh. He knew that he had assisted in the downfall of Chiquita. He was glad when Starlight took the child and went away and left him alone with his dead. There beside the dead Chiquita he abandoned himself to remorse. The shock he had suffered caused him to think—something he had not done since the night when he beheld Chiquita for the first time. There upon his knees he vowed that he would devote his time, and strength, and talent to Wawa, Chiquita's child, and the

Indian race. "Dr. Nachita is right; it rests with the few educated Indians—the destiny of the race. Shall they rescue themselves from the slavery of ignorance, of vice, of idleness? From this hour I devote myself to their cause, and time will tell." At nine o'clock on the following morning Tonto, Wawa and Starlight rode alone behind the hearse that carried the remains of the once beautiful and famous woman who had given up fame and luxury for the man she loved, to later learn that self-preservation is the first law of nature—that when assailed by physical suffering, disappointments, poverty and want, her love could not survive. That when she changed, love flew away, and in that hour the consciousness of what she might have been, of what she once really longed to be, seared and tortured her soul. As they turned from the grave, the trembling lips of Tonto whispered to the child of Chiquita: "How cruel—the injustice of the pale face. Dr. Nachita is right! We must overcome prejudice; we must master fate; we must stand on an equal footing with the best of men. Looking back I see that the general good should be our highest aim. Starlight has found the better way. From this hour I give my all to the welfare of Wawa and my race."

When the carriage stopped with a jolt that awakened Tonto from his dreaming, the child had fallen asleep upon the breast of Starlight.

CHAPTER XXII

The Home Coming

Here on the gray and purple slopes,
Above the silver streams,
We watch the crimson sunset weave
Its colors through our dreams.

A solitary couple alighted from the Santa Fe train one glorious morning, in a small mining town at the foot of the mountains, in the far West. The man appeared at home —upon familiar ground—for he strode along through the village with careless step, and his smile was that of the child. His massive head and shoulders resembled the mountain lion. His dusky skin and shock of heavy black hair suggested the mineral of that rock-ribbed, lava-encrusted region. His large face and great black eyes beamed with intelligence and good humor. He led the way, followed closely by a pale-faced woman who blinked her deep-set blue eyes in the flood of sunlight that bathed the earth. Dr. Nachita and Blue Bird had reached the land of their dreams. "Come on! Come on! We must take the trail right now. Later in the day the heat is severe and I am impatient; right down there, beyond the blacksmith shop, we get the ponies; see that shed yonder?" "It is no trouble to see in this light," Blue Bird replied. The doctor continued, "On our way to the plateau I will see Chief Ugly Bear. I must talk with the old chief regarding matters of great importance to his tribe." They had mounted the ponies and were riding across "the desert" when the doctor forgot the Indians for a moment and said: "Look there, Blue Bird; that is the barrel cactus; it contains a watery pulp and the Indians never suffered from thirst if they could reach that plant. They just cut into it and scooped up the moist pulp with their hands. Now, Blue Bird, observe most plants in this locality have stickers or spines to protect them from the birds and animals; wonderful provision where food is scarce. Look there, Blue Bird, that is an ocotillo; in the spring time its tips bear flame-colored blossoms." They approached a narrow valley. "Look there, Blue Bird; that tall bush with the long green spikes is the paloverde, and here is the cat-claw with its little curved thorn and fragrant yellow blossoms; remember that, Blue Bird, for most blossoms in this region are scentless. Now, right over there you see yuccas or soap weed; in the spring time they are full of cream-white flowers." "The plants and the grass all look very queer to me, like another world. And where are the Indians?" Blue Bird asked. "Right now I see the old chief's lodge by that clump of willow," the doctor replied. "Now you stay here, Blue Bird, and hunt flowers while I ride down to the river and speak with the Chief Ugly Bear." He pointed off to the right where a long, thin streak of smoke ascended from the bank. He rode away and Blue Bird was soon lost in contemplation of the shrubs and bright-plumaged birds.

Ugly Bear sat upon the ground mending a weather-beaten harness, when Dr. Nachita rode up. "Well! Well!" and "Ha o" were the high lights of their salutation. They conversed in low guarded tones; words came slowly to their lips and were enunciated with marked deliberation. "Let's see, this is Wednesday; send out the riders, call them together here. right here, late in the afternoon of Friday. Don't forget the mescal bake. My! My! This home coming is a red letter day in my life. I go now; to-morrow I come back." With these words Dr. Nachita left Chief Ugly Bear who gazed after horse and rider with a look of deep admiration in his jet black eyes. Then Ugly Bear straightened his tall figure and slowly said: "He heap good Indian! Heap big Indian talk fine; come back to-morrow." When Dr. Nachita and Blue Bird began to climb the rocky trail that led to the mesa, a tense, somber expression settled upon the doctor's face. Blue Bird was silent; she feared disturbing him when his eyes closed in just that peculiar way. On, up toward the sky they climbed, here and there hugging the rocky wall, just a few feet from an open abyss. They knew that only the unfailing instinct of the ponies separated them from eternity; to slip or stumble would mean death. At one of these points the doctor said, "Here, Blue Bird, one lies naked before God. Here a man shrivels to the dimensions of a partridge. You feel small, in fact, you know that you are small. The marts of trade make a man conceited and boastful; that is man's world—of his making. Here the folks vegetate in God's world. Everything strikes the same level, as it were; the people live on the same plane with the birds and squirrels and skunks." Blue Bird became restless. "I call this hard climbing; nothing easy about this," she said in a frightened voice. "Nothing of the sort; you make it hard work; all in your mind, Blue Bird. Depend upon the pony. Whoa, Bill! Steady, there! Blue Bird objects to being tumbled off the cliff like a common boulder; let us keep to the trail; I have work to accomplish. There now, I told you—no cause for worry." They had reached the top of the plateau. Overhead the deep blue sky seemed very near; so close it frightened Blue Bird. The air was marvellously clean and fresh and the stillness awed them. He tethered the ponies to a rock, and Dr. Nachita led the way to the far edge of the mesa, and there spread out before their eyes, far down below lay a green fertile valley dotted over with houses, flocks of sheep, and herds of cattle, orchards and vineyards. On either side of the valley rose abruptly, high rocky walls. Toward the west the mass projected itself out into the valley in finger-like ridges, as though a great hand had been held out over the valley, and the spread fingers had turned to stone. "Down there, Blue Bird, is the spot where my tribe once lived —in that Garden of Eden, but see the long slender shadows reaching out over the valley from those stone fingers! Ah, the shadows fell upon my race—upon my own family; I recall vaguely that black night. All were gathered about the camp fire close to the grass hut; a hostile band crept upon us; then it was all dark and confusion reigned, and I realized that I was being carried away, and through my child brain ran the stories I had been told of the power the enemy possessed to change little boys into dogs, cats, or toads. My! My! Blue Bird, fear is terrible. It is a crime to teach fear. Well! Well! That is past long ago. Right there, Blue Bird, where I am pointing, I picked up the hand-mill we have in the 'den,' the two flat stones for grinding grass seeds and grains." "How did they treat their women?" Blue Bird asked. "The woman was the whole thing," promptly replied the doctor. "Well, I hear about her driving and hitching the horses—" "O, yes," he interrupted, "she harnessed the horse because the horse belonged to her. The Indian sat in the rear of the wagon, because that was where he belonged. The Indian was all bedecked and bespangled, Blue Bird, because the woman who loved him thus adored him; because it pleased her own fancy. She selected and chose, and honored and adored her mate, but her choice once made, she belonged absolutely to that mate. Our young men were timid; I could never in my boyhood days speak to a woman. To enter a ballroom or reception hall. My! I could never endure the ordeal. They would stare at me—someone might be ashamed of me. A strange sensitiveness kept me in fear of the white man's curiosity—the smile of disdain. I was an Indian—to be stared at, considered queer, that is terrible, but we must endure. I found wonderful friends. I could meet them in my own den, away from prying eyes; but let us keep to the present. My soul drinks in the beauty and grandeur of the scene before me, and I thank God for all that is good and beautiful; and yet I cannot forget the poor remnant of my race. Their faces are sad; they walk about in fear. They cannot even manage their own home affairs; they must get permission to exist. I will not keep still! I will be heard! I have a right to demand justice and I have a right to call out to my people to arouse themselves and claim the best that this life offers, instead of waiting and drifting, and all the time slipping off the earth. Blue Bird, man must have an atmosphere, and reason."

"Would you care to live here always, in sight of the things that remind you of the past?" Blue Bird asked naively.

"No! No!" he replied, "this is wild and grand and picturesque, and I love to come back. I just must come back for short periods, but when a man has once known the comforts of a well-ordered home, he could never again endure life in a grass hut, and then, Blue Bird, to be able to reach up as I do, and take from a convenient shelf a bound volume, open its covers and come into close touch with the soul of a Hugo, a Shakespeare, an Emerson. My! My! Blue Bird, no man could give up such opportunities for this life of simple rustic stagnation. Think of not being able to read and write—just make your mark! No! No! Here everything is in the crude; no evolution; no progress. The whole environment of the reservation Indian favors stagnation, decay, death. They just drift on, close to earth like birds with clipped wings. They have all the inate material possessed by any race, but they have been hypnotized into a state of inertia. They have had someone to think for them, these many years, and they have been going backward. They are sick people, Blue Bird, but they will recover. They wronged themselves when first they took into their souls hate and bitterness. The Indians were wronged many times; many times; but hate and bitterness destroy the soul; the price is too great. My heart rebels against the present status of the Indians. I am tortured by their sorrows. Each day their misery prods deeper into my soul."

High above the gold and green valley he stood erect. Toward the clouds he lifted his hands and cried, "My God! Help me to rescue my people! I am dumb! I am helpless!" "Why not let them remain as they are?" Blue Bird whispered. "This excitement is not good; let us go down where you cannot see so much that hurts you; I came to see birds, and flowers and baskets, and eat mescal. I thought you would give up raving about Indians when you were away from the books, and could talk with them, but you have put on the loud pedal since we arrived; come along; I am going." She mounted her pony and started down. He feared she might lose her way alone on the crooked trail. He mounted, cast a long lingering glance over the beautiful valley; at the walls of rock and the shadows that lengthened while he lingered; then turned away with eyes wet with tears, to follow Blue Bird down the winding trail. Once, upon a level stretch of path, he paused and repeated the song of Elsie Jewell, the daughter of his friend Rev. Silas Sheldon:

"O Arizona, land of mine:
Thou holdest charms of every clime;
From deserts wild to heights sublime;
O Arizona, land of mine.

"I'll ne'er forget thy deserts wild,
For here I lived as nature's child."

CHAPTER XXIII

The Tocsin

Chief Ugly Bear's runners had called the people to his lodge. Some had traveled many miles to hear the message of Dr. Nachita, a full-blooded Indian who had grown up with the pale face: an Indian who held a university degree and a medical degree. Chief Ugly Bear lived in an isolated spot upon the bank of a river that poured out from a narrow canyon near by. About his lodge several families had camped. Clumps of tall brush and broad willows clung to the river bank, and the ground was covered by a rank growth of coarse grass. Toward the east stretched low sand dunes, dotted with sage brush and cacti. An audience tent had been erected near the lodge of the chief. Long, straight poles had been set in the ground and roofed over with brush and grass. The Indians came on foot; in wagons, or riding ponies. Beneath the rude tent they sat down upon the bare ground in semi-circles; outside they sat close to, or beneath their wagons and beside the bushes that they might escape the direct rays of the hot sun. Blue Bird was beside the wife of Chief Ugly Bear. There was not much conversation, and that little was in cautious, low tones, suggesting fear or, perhaps impending danger. A rude table was placed at one end of the tent; Chief Ugly Bear sat behind the table with half a dozen full-bloods, all dignified, intelligent, proud men past middle life, all counselors of the tribe. When Dr. Nachita stepped out in front of the table, a few Indians seated far out, stood up that they might better see the man who would speak to them through an interpreter. A grave stillness settled upon the people huddled about him. When Dr. Nachita looked into their faces and struggled with his pent-up emotions. He stood thus, looking straight into their dark eyes, and then away into the blue sky for a long time. Then slowly the words came from his lips in short explosive sentences: "My people! Hear me! Think well! I have much to say. I come far to counsel with you. Day and night I ponder over the question, the future—what does it hold for my race?" He paused, while a tall, dark Indian beside him interpreted. They nodded in assent, and the doctor continued: "When I came last time I asked permission from the superintendent to speak to you; this was denied me. To-day I am speaking without permission, because I believe that the Creator gave me the right to uphold truth and justice; to lift my voice in the interest of those who need help. You may not agree with me on all matters, but remember my heart is with my race. I believe that I grasp the viewpoint of both the white man and the Indian. Now! The point is this: Are you content with the present conditions of reservation life? Is the Government satisfied with the progress you are making?" The faces turned toward Dr. Nachita were stern and sad. There were mutterings and grunts, and then death-like stillness as he continued: "They have trained the Indian under the reservation system for a long, long time, understand, but no one seems pleased with the results. They find fault continually with the Indian, never with the system. Why, a cat, or dog, or bird can be trained if the method is correct. In getting results all depends upon having the right method, understand? Well! Now! What does all this mean? Simply that the reservation system is all wrong. To reserve means to set aside, to place by itself, to segregate, and so, understand, the Indian living on the reservation, reserves the old thoughts, the old traditions, the old hatred, the old suspicion and all the old things that the pale face wants him to get rid of, understand?" Here the interpreter had some difficulty, after which Dr. Nachita continued, "All individuals, all races advance along the same lines. All development, all betterment must come through better thinking; through a better understanding of natural laws that govern all life. Our race must advance along the same trail the pale face has traveled. All things develop from within. Nature makes no distinction, understand; the same laws apply to all races regardless of color or location. We do not remain stationary; we go forward or backward. This is the law; all life is motion; we must choose which way we will go. Right here my heart cries out to you—forget the past! It is not a question of what once was; nor a question of what might have been; it is what may be done at the present time to improve conditions. While my race have remained silent, impassive, immovable, nursing hate and revenge, the great world has swept on, and on. Forget every wrong associated with the past—understand, we must forget. This is one of the great lessons learned by the pale face." For several minutes the interpreter struggled with both languages, and thanked his stars that he had not forgotten the native tongue. At last Dr. Nachita resumed his address with great vehemence: "Environment is not fixed and unchangeable. A man's environment may be changed; there is no law against this, understand; and when environment hinders normal, healthy development, it is time for a change. The reservation system has been operating for more than fifty years. Who is satisfied with results? The Indian? No! The Government? No! Surely something is wrong! The root of the trouble lies in segregation. The fact that I must speak to you through an interpreter, at the end of fifty years of reservation life, is proof that little progress is being made toward real American citizenship. Something is wrong with the system, or my people would speak and understand English." The keen, alert old Indians shook their heads and looked in the direction of the trail; fear looked out from their faces. Dr. Nachita continued in lowered tones: "This fear I see in your faces confirms the fact that you do not consider yourselves free people. I stand here a living demonstration of the fact that the Indian can be educated if the method is correct, understand. In the hospitals we see the rigid application of the system, regardless of results. The discipline must be maintained, if the patients all die. The rules are eternal, unchangeable. The pneumonia patient on being admitted must have a bath; of course no well-trained nurse could take charge of an unbathed patient. The poor victim is exposed, scrubbed, *rubbed,* and dies because too weak to stand it. Work—and more work is the panacea for the troubled heart, the idle brain, the empty purse, change the atmosphere of the home, make it fit for the presence of deities. Home is the foundation of all citizenship, good or bad. That child or adult who does not have daily association with the best people, the best books, the best amusements; who does not have the best food for the nutrition of the body, the best thoughts for the nutrition of the mind—that child or adult is badly handicapped in the race for knowledge, success, honor and life! Forget all else and bear this well in mind. Go out and teach the pale face that the Indian of history is a phantom. Teach the world that you are like all men. That you are capable, sensitive, alert, loyal, honest, thinking human beings, ready to accept all that is useful in the building of noble bodies and noble characters. My heart aches and my nights are sleepless. I must fight back my tears when I behold the white man's picture of my people. I beg you to shake off your fear and lethargy, your hate and resentfulness and accept your own. All the noble qualities are yours. Do not hide them; do not smother them by superstition and ignorance; free the mind. Demand for your children the highest and best; go out and obtain these gifts by hard, patient labor and concentration. Nothing comes of sitting still. Awake! And mount upward to the high places where the air is pure and the sun shines all day above the clouds.

"A change is coming, but old systems die hard, remember; this was the case when our race was compelled to give up the old life. Find yourselves as I found myself, through education and association with thinking men and women. The greatest service that it is possible to render to child or man is to teach them to think. I beg you to think out your own problems, and when you do this you will recognize the value and importance of education. Why, my dear friends, the companionship and inspiration of one single good book is worth twenty years of lazy, aimless life as a ward of the government. Of course, understand, the government never aimed to bring about this result, but the system works out in this way. My race possess all the material, all the possibilities possessed by any race. There is no dream of fame, or wealth or power, that has come true in the lives of any individual or race, that is not possible for you, but not in your present environment. Come out into the world away from these pest houses, and be the noble, useful men and women that I know you can be. Some will fall by the wayside, but that is true of all races. The weak perish. You will be compelled to work or starve, understand; but this is true even of the wild animals. Work is noble; labor is the only road to success. I ask each man, each woman of Indian blood to refuse charity! Refuse charity! It weakens the whole character. Work for the education that you see the pale face using as a lever to success. Work for the development of noble character and physical perfection. Be a factor in the onward movement of the world. But this is impossible for segregated Indians. There is no inspiration toward effort of any sort. You are supervised; someone does the thinking for you, and you all go in the direction of least resistance, understand? Now, this attitude was not possible for me. Why? Because the environment was not favorable to such results. I did as the majority did. I went with the tide, and now I know that all the Indian requires is the proper tide. I would have you demand a final settlement with the United States Government regarding land and money, and then I would have you go out, and take up your individual burdens as all men and women of every race must do, if they would survive. Preparing the Indian for citizenship? Bosh! Nonsense! The Indian must prepare himself for citizenship, which means simply to understand his obligations and relations to others. The reservation does not favor the qualities necessary to citizenship. Reservation life fosters dependence—idleness, deceit, ignorance, depravity, illness, idiocy. Those who escape these conditions are the strong characters. Now, understand! Because of these conditions the tendency is backward—always backward. We cannot remain motionless. All life necessitates some form of motion. Stagnation is death. The apathy that has crept upon my people wrings my heart. I beseech you, do not accept the idle, vapid, carefree existence of wardship. To the Indian the world belongs as much as to the white man, and every Indian should take up his share of responsibility; but that cannot be so long as the Indians are supervised. My friends, fear nothing; come out into the world and demonstrate the bravery of our race by struggling for all that is best and noblest. The Indians should have the best that life affords. Why not? At the same time I beg you —reject the vices of the pale face; spurn everything that weakens. Hate sears and blackens like fire. I know that the Indians as a mass—understand, are ready to recognize the restraints of civilization; those who are not, must suffer the lash of the law just as the pale face. The whole reservation system has a tendency to breed deception, injustice, weakness, ignorance and disease. The Indian children should attend the public schools. That is the place to learn citizenship. Every Indian, young or old, should speak and write the English language because it is the official language of this great commonwealth. Any individual who cannot speak the language of the country in which he lives is sadly handicapped. The whole system is wrong. Fifty years of wardship and still many Indians cannot speak English! Still making their mark! Think of it! Is it not time for a radical change? The principle of reservation life is wrong. 'To coerce; to limit; to coddle; to deceive; to help feed and clothe never will produce real manhood and womanhood.' The system was planned for the protection of the Indians, but results are not satisfactory; the system should be abolished. The colored children are in the public schools—why not the Indian children? When given the proper environment I believe that my race will advance more rapidly than have other races, but if for want of supervision my people will lay down and die—as some dear people think—then let my people die. I know the white man's life and I know reservation life, and I say in the name of reason, and justice, come away from these unsightly places! Come out into full daylight! I must speak; I must cry out! I owe a debt to my people; I will not go my way and abandon my race; if need be, I will die for the cause. I am weary of the slurs cast upon my people—I, who know their possibilities! The history of the American Indian is a sad, sad story, a terrible tragedy, a misunderstanding that results in injustice, bitterness, hate, despair and death." The doctor recognized a slight commotion outside the tent toward the east. Several Indians stood up and peered into the darkness, for night had descended. Those who looked out along the trail did not see but heard the approach of horses. Dr. Nachita had ceased to speak; he felt the alarm of those about him, and stood motionless. The Indians drew close and signaled for him to escape, but he stood quietly looking into their eyes, when the circle parted and two tall lank Indian policemen shambled up to him. One held a scrap of dirty paper which he flourished in the doctor's face. The other grasped him by the arm and growled: "Come along; you go to jail. Agent say lock him up; he no have permit; he no ask me to speak; agent run this place." "Very well, I will go," the doctor answered. "The agent has the authority and power to imprison me; an Indian cannot speak his mind or defend himself. Think of it! And this is our native land!" The two policemen hustled him out upon the trail and they rode away into the black night. For a little time no one stirred among the group of Indians left behind; then an old blind man said: "Ugh! Big doctor too much white man; talk heap lot. Agent good; agent give me tobac—agent all right." A group of young Indians surged out along the road with a sudden impulse to rescue Dr. Nachita, when suddenly the reservation agent dashed into their midst with half a dozen Indian policemen at his heels. Dismounting, he shouted: "You Indians, clear out for your homes, and be quick about it! Every Indian found hanging around here will be locked up; I'll stand no nonsense! Clear out, I tell you!" They scattered like ants. An old squaw stumbled over an object lying at her feet; she bent down and found Blue Bird upon the ground, her face half buried in the sand. "Come along! He lock you up too," she muttered, as she shook the limp form. Other Indians came and raised the prostrate woman; they questioned, and begged her to arouse herself, but no sound came from her lips. "Carry that woman into the lodge of Ugly Bear," the agent commanded. They lifted the body instantly the command was given. They carried Blue Bird into the grass hut, and very gently laid her down upon the bare ground. The agency physician was summoned and fear settled upon each dusky face, for Blue Bird was dead. Dazed and helpless, they looked into each other's eyes and waited in silence. It was very dark and still within and without. A few moments of terrible suspense and then a shot rang out. A bullet whizzed through the still air, and there before the lodge of Chief Ugly Bear, upon the ground lay the agent writhing and clutching with both hands his side, where a bullet had entered. Two policemen bore him quickly away, and to a trusty runner Chief Ugly Bear whispered, "Go, get word to Starlight and Tonto! Dr. Nachita say they good friends. Go!" And the Redman vanished into the night.

CHAPTER XXIV

The Alarm

To Starlight the message came: "Dr. Nachita in jail; Blue Bird dead; agent wounded; speak for us." For the moment Starlight was deprived of speech and motion, but when the shock had passed and she grasped the meaning of its few words she crumpled the message in her hand and ran to the big theater where at that very hour Tonto sang. As she sped along the street she heard newsboys crying, "Extra! Extra! All about the Indian uprising!" Past them she ran with her black hair flying about her shoulders. From a street corner a man shouted, "There goes one of them pesky Indians!" But Starlight rushed on like the wind. When she reached his side Tonto was about to step out before the footlights. "Tonto! Tonto!" she cried and grasped him by the arm. "Tell them the truth about the Indians! Speak for Dr. Nachita! I fear for him!" With affright Tonto looked into Starlight's wild eyes. Starlight so calm and self-possessed—Starlight crying out in this manner? What could it mean? He took from her hand the message. He could not believe his eyes; something seemed wrong with his brain. Dazed and trembling he hurried out upon the stage and spoke to the audience. "Wait a little, friends; I cannot sing; something has happened in the West; my friend, the Indian Doctor Nachita is in jail, this message tells me. One is dead and one is wounded. I do not understand; there must be some blunder, some mistake. I do not know what this means, but Dr. Nachita has done no wrong. I know that he has wronged no one. He is bold for the truth about the Indian. He has planned no wrong. He has just one thought and that is the welfare of our race—the Indian people. He loves even dumb animals. The Indians could not rise up and claim their freedom; they are too much weakened. I fear harm will come to Dr. Nachita." An intoxicated man bellowed from the balcony: "We know all about the Indians! Send the militia after them and finish the job!" A great uproar started; angry voices were heard from every direction, when a tall man with silver gray locks came upon the stage, lifted his hands and called: "Attention, fellow citizens! The Indian is a man! The Indian is a human being! The Indian is my brother!" He clasped the hand of Tonto and continued: "I am here to protect his rights. No harm will befall Dr. Nachita. I will throw the entire weight of my influence against it, for I know this man, Dr. Nachita. I have had the privilege of witnessing the kindness, the nobility and the fine sense of justice possessed by Dr. Nachita, and I am ready to defend his name and his race." He led Starlight before the footlights, but nothing could be heard, for a great roar of applause swept back and forth across the big theater. Toward the audience Starlight and Tonto lifted their faces, wet with tears, and began to sing, "America." Every voice in the great auditorium mingled with the voices of the Indians. From the balcony the intoxicated man shouted, "Wire Washington! Turn loose the doctor," and later, it was done, in Judge Thoroughgood's smooth, technical, courteous way. Upon the following day as Tonto and Starlight were about to go to Dr. Nachita's aid, a message came telling them that he was free and would return to the city; "Wait there" was his command.

The body of Blue Bird was laid to rest amidst the scenes of his tragic childhood. "I shall come back," he said. "My heart is here; but at the present time I must give my time, my strength, my all toward the uprooting of prejudice against the Indian. It is all a sad misunderstanding. I love the Indian and I love the pale face. Why can we not both be men and citizens on common ground? Why can we not understand each other? There is room for all! I must not grow bitter—this awful tragedy I must forget! I must forget! I must struggle on for the universal good of my people, and not even ask to see the way one hour beyond the present; it is a sad, sad story—the Indian story." And then he fell to dreaming, with closed eyes, in silence, while the train sped on and on toward the great metropolis—his home.

The agency superintendent recovered and made a hasty exit from the reservation. His old bravado was gone, and in its place he held a sneaking fear of the Indian when aroused, or compelled to defend himself.

CHAPTER XXV

"The Dawn"

Before an elegant desk, in a well-furnished office on one of the busiest streets of the city, we find Starlight. Her manner has lost the old imperialism that marked her college days. She is more beautiful; less haughty and scornful toward the pale face. The loss of bitterness, and the unfolding of a new love has wrought a magic change, and those who now meet Starlight say, "She is a perfect queen; an all around educated, cultured, talented young woman of great promise; if only the women of her race will follow her lead, their transition is accomplished." On the plate glass window of Starlight's office the passer-by might read, " 'The Dawn,' a Journal devoted to the American Indian." Upon a table close to the window were piled copies of the journal whose forward proclamation ran thus: "Starlight descended from the bravest of our brave men. 'The Dawn' represents the great interests of our race. Patriotism, sociology, science, economics, and art for the Indian is our slogan. Starlight is the first Indian woman to step into the limelight of journalism. Indians, lend your aid; send in your best thoughts, if they concern the progress of the Red Man. Help to break down prejudice, and proclaim our principles; our ideals; and our worth. All who have been sad and silent, turn your faces toward 'The Dawn' and lift up your voices. Starlight has struggled through the long, dark night. She lights our way toward the dawn." Down the street with a companion came Mat Bulldowney. He stopped before the window and read the new sign. To his friend he said: "Be gorry! an' what in the name of hiven means this? What's goin' on wid the Indians? Wakin' up, maybe; givin' up blankets an' beads an' baskets an' goin' to printin' papers, eh? Edicatin' they do be after sayin' that's goin' some. I thot the Indin men kept their wimmin in their proper spere. Wil, I'm one what's glad one of their wimmin has broke loose. Shure I'll take her magazine; that tepee business, an' bells an' feathers an' warhoop an' sich stuff always did get me. When I was a by I trailed after them Indian shows regular an' be gorry, me mother says I'd behave fur most a hull day when the show wuz in town, providin' she'd come across wid the price of a ticket. Here one of thim bloomin' red-skins is blossomin' out as an editress. Be gorry, the world do move sure, an' all by Starlight." Matt left his comrade, stepped inside, paid a year's subscription, took from the hand of Starlight a copy of "The Dawn," a receipt and a queenly smile. She long ago had learned the value of correct language and manners. Matt soon found that his command of English precluded a clear understanding of the high-grade articles published in "The Dawn," all of which had been written by Indians. "Well, I can't read the bloomin' stuff an' believe me I'm niver a goin' to night school to ketch up wid Indians. Starlight an' Moonlight be hanged" was his final apostrophe, as he slammed the journal down upon the sitting-room table in his boarding house.

Tonto, who was one of the leading contributors to the journal, also had acquitted himself with honor. He had finished his course in law and was winning many legal cases for the Indians. He would only accept cases founded upon an appeal for simple justice. He constantly held before the people the cause of justice for his race. He, too, was battering down prejudice with manly conduct, and displacing darkness with light, and error with truth. He compelled attention and respect from the pale face. To him had come a vision of better, nobler days for the Indian, and he had accepted his part of the responsibility. He knew that the eyes of the world were upon his people and that prejudice was giving way to confidence. He said to Starlight, "Dr. Nachita is right; the few leaders must hold up the torches until the masses arrive. The renaissance of our race is at hand."

CHAPTER XXVI

THE RENDEZVOUS AT TWILIGHT

Dr. Nachita returned to his home broken in health. The fire and whirlwind of former days had all disappeared. Patients came and were turned away. The doctor was ill, too ill to see them. He pleaded continuously for Starlight and Tonto, and Wawa, his namesake. "Come," he said, "come and maake my home your own. So far as I know I have no relatives upon this earth. I adopt you all as my children. I long for your presence each moment." And so they went to his home and after a few days Judge Thoroughgood came and the little Wawa was legally adopted by Dr. Nachita. "I must have a legal heir," he said. Through the long sleepless nights Tonto or Starlight watched beside him and buoyed up his strength with a devotion that was stronger to help than any potion. They held long councils on Indian affairs, and especially the marriage of Starlight and Tonto. "This I desire next to the general welfare of my people," the doctor pleaded, "send for Judge Thoroughgood; have him come at sunset when the light pours into my room in a flood of glory; that is the hour." And so the old judge came, and there in the lodge surrounded by the dusky mementoes and the sad Indian faces upon the walls, all gilded with crimson light, Starlight and Tonto were wedded. Dr. Nachita held the little Wawa by the hand, and the old nurse stood in the curtained doorway while the judge with the silver-gray locks, slowly read the marriage service. When it was over and Starlight bent down and kissed the forehead of Dr. Nachita, he murmured: "It is well! It is well! The future of our race I leave with you, my children! As leaders, understand, there must be leaders. I am happy, for I know that you will never flinch or falter; that you will stand for truth and justice. Lead our women, Starlight; much depends upon their enlightenment." And then he fell asleep; but when the first gray morning light crept into the room, after hours of pain, he called for Starlight and commanded that she should send for the Indian friends, "those who think as I think—call them now; do not delay, Starlight, tell the friends to come to me." Starlight glided from the room with a rapid, agile movement peculiar to her race when danger threatens. Dr. Nachita lay with closed eyes, silently awaiting his loyal comrades, and that specter all meet some place along the trail. At times he dreamed of his own tragic childhood, of "being torn up by the roots," he had often said, "and transplanted into strange, new soil." He battled with powerful enemies, or he climbed the zigzag path by the mesa overlooking the green valley, and Blue Bird was beside him. He heard sweet voices singing, and weird sounds from strange instruments. He awoke and called feebly to Starlight: "I hear the Liebestraum; I hear it just as Madam Yetta played it that night, with the lights turned low. Wonderful! Wonderful! See that the Indians get the knowledge that will enable them to express the music in their souls—it is there, understand." By and by the Indians came one by one, and stood with bowed heads beside his bed. He called each name and greeted them with a faint smile. "Take me into the den, Starlight," he whispered; "I must see again those sad reminders of our past. I must see them again; I will be better then." Great strong arms lifted him tenderly and slowly bore him into the lodge filled with dull color and somber shadows and faded treasures. In one corner of the great davenport Starlight placed an armful of soft pillows, and there the Indians laid him down with a tenderness that brought tears into the eyes of the old judge who was waiting there with Tonto and the child. When Judge Thoroughgood bent low and clasped his hand Dr. Nachita asked: "What of the future?" "I see a bright sky," the judge replied. "Devotion such as yours will not pass unrewarded;

it wins respect; it is a power for good; it clears away prejudice; it makes the future bright with hope." Dr. Nachita closed his eyes and lay as though asleep. Then suddenly he raised himself to a half upright position and said in low tones, "Come close, my children, Wawa, Starlight, Tonto, come close. My mantle falls upon you. Never, never give up until our race is free from every bar to their progress. The Indian Bureau, understand, means segregation; segregation means deterioration. Tell the Indians to compel recognition from the world by honest, earnest, faithful effort." He turned to the child sitting beside him. "If only I could pass on to him my experience, my knowledge and my belief in the future of my people—he is the morning, I am the night—he comes as I depart. I cannot see, come close, Starlight." They knelt beside him—Starlight and Tonto. They took his cold hands and pressed them against their warm breasts. He whispered, "Tell my people—to think—my people—tell them—to think—tell them to think—understand—to think—" His head sank down into the soft pillows. The little group of Indians stood in silence, trembling. They heard Starlight's low sobbing but they could not see her face, for night had fallen and the room was dark.